I will give you a new heart and put a new spirit within you; I will take the heart of stone out of your flesh and give you a heart of flesh.

EZEKIEL 36:26 NKJV

THE 100
MOST IMPORTANT
BIBLE VERSES

Presented to:

Pauline Ricketts

Presented by:

Pauline Francis

Date:

12 - 13 - 06

Test all things;
hold fast what is good.

1 Thessalonians 5:21 NKJV

THE 100
MOST IMPORTANT
BIBLE VERSES

W PUBLISHING GROUP
A Division of Thomas Nelson Publishers
Since 1798

www.wpublishinggroup.com

The 100 Most Important Bible Verses
©2005 by GRQ, Inc.
Brentwood, Tennessee 37027

Published by W Publishing Group, a Division of Thomas Nelson, Inc., P.O. Box 141000, Nashville, Tennessee 37214.

W Publishing Group books may be purchased in bulk for educational, business, fundraising, or sales promotional use. For information, please email SpecialMarkets@ThomasNelson.com.

Scripture quotations are from the following sources:

• The New Century Version® (NCV). Copyright © 1987, 1988, 1991 by Word Publishing, a Division of Thomas Nelson, Inc. Used by permission. All rights reserved.
• The New King James Version® (NKJV), copyright © 1979, 1980, 1982, Thomas Nelson, Inc., Publishers.• The Holy Bible, New International Version (NIV). Copyright © 1973, 1978, 1984, International Bible Society. Used by permission of Zondervan Bible Publishers. • New Living Translation (NLT), copyright © 1996 by Tyndale House Publishers, Inc., Wheaton, Ill. All rights reserved. • The Message (MSG), copyright © 1993. Used by permission of NavPress Publishing Group.

Managing Editor: Lila Empson
Associate Editor: Laura Kendall
Manuscript: Vicki J. Kuyper
Design: Thatcher Design, Nashville, Tennessee

Library of Congress Cataloging-in-Publication Data

100 most important Bible verses.
    p. cm.
ISBN 0-8499-0027-1
1. Bible—Quotations. I. Title: One hundred most important Bible verses. II. W Publishing Group.
BS416.A15 2005
220.5'2—dc22

20050100083

Printed in China.
06 07 08 — 9 8 7 6 5 4

God's word is alive and working and is sharper than a double-edged sword. It cuts all the way into us, where the soul and the spirit are joined, to the center of our joints and bones. And it judges the thoughts and feelings in our hearts.

HEBREWS 4:12 NCV

Contents

Your word is a lamp to my feet and a
light to my path.

PSALM 119:105 NKJV

Introduction

Reading the Bible from cover to cover can seem like
a daunting task. After all, the Bible is a big book that
doesn't read like an ordinary book. That's because the
Bible is anything but ordinary. It's a love letter from God
to the world. Instead of having a beginning, a middle, and
an end, the Bible tells an ongoing story, one in which you
play an important part.

The 100 Most Important Bible Verses is designed to help you get better acquainted with God and his words one step at a time. Each brief chapter focuses on a bite-size portion of the Bible. You can discover more about the cultural, historical, and scriptural context of the verse, as well as gain insight into the verse's underlying theme and life-changing truth. You will also find ideas on how to apply what you learn to how you live.

No verse in the Bible can stand alone without the support of every word God has provided. However, by reading *The 100 Most Important Bible Verses*, you'll get an overview of what the Bible has to say. It will help you better know where to turn when you need to hear what God says about a specific topic, such as contentment, love, problems, or peace. May *The 100 Most Important Bible Verses* help you know more about the Bible and its author in a deeper and more relevant way.

Jesus said, "Your Father knows the things you need before you ask him."

MATTHEW 6:8 NCV

Father Knows Best

Jesus gave his disciples the Lord's Prayer as an example of how to pray. Right before he spoke those famous words, Jesus shared a few reasons *why* one should pray. To do this, he provided two examples—negative ones. Jesus said the Pharisees prayed in public because they wanted to be seen as holy by other people. He also said idol worshipers prayed, repeating themselves over and over, because they believed that the more frequently they asked for something, the better chance they had of having their request granted. After those negative examples, Jesus spoke the reassurance that God already knows what you need.

At first, his words may seem to provide a reason why *not* to pray, instead of why to pray. If God knows what you need before you ask, why bother asking in the first place? Jesus's point is, the purpose of prayer isn't to be noticed by other people—or even by God. God already notices you. He knows everything about you and your life. Prayer is not a way to draw God's attention to your needs. It is a way to draw your attention to how much you need God.

Your greatest continual need is to better know and love God. Communicating with him about the details of your life keeps you aware of how involved he already is. It also helps you see how many of your needs

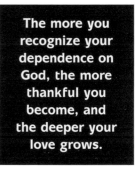

The more you recognize your dependence on God, the more thankful you become, and the deeper your love grows.

he fills every day. The more you recognize your dependence on God, the more thankful you become, and the deeper your love grows.

The Lord's Prayer teaches you to pray for your daily bread. Jesus's words from Matthew don't contradict that lesson. They're a reminder that God needs to be involved in your life, not merely informed about it.

If we confess our sins, He is faithful and just to forgive us our sins and to cleanse us from all unrighteousness.

1 JOHN 1:9 NKJV

Fully Forgiven

Being a scapegoat is not a job most people would volunteer for. After all, it implies taking the blame for what others have done. But in the Old Testament, God offered forgiveness to his people in exactly this way. The priest would lay his hands on the head of a goat and symbolically transfer onto the scapegoat the blame for the sins the people had committed. The priest then sent the animal into the wilderness to take the people's offenses far away. Once the scapegoat removed the people's sins, God in his holiness could once again draw near to the people he loved.

In the New Testament, a different kind of scapegoat appeared—Jesus Christ. As God's Son, he willingly chose to bear the offenses of the whole world, to take the blame for everything the people had done against God since the dawn of time and until the end of it. Jesus was innocent of the sins and transgresions of the people, and yet, as the scapegoat, he took the punishment for them all so that his beloved people could be spared.

The great hope and promise of this verse is that it tells you exactly what you need to do to allow Jesus to be your scapegoat, which opens the door to God's forgiveness in your life. *To confess* simply means "to agree." Take a few moments each day to agree with God about how well your thoughts,

Move forward with confidence, fully forgiven and free from guilt.

words, and actions have lined up with what he desires for your life. Move forward with confidence, fully forgiven and free from guilt.

Once God forgives you, all traces of your past offenses are gone. His forgiveness wipes away any feelings of guilt or blame.

We know that all things work together for good to those who love God, to those who are the called according to His purpose.

ROMANS 8:28 NKJV

More Than Meets the Eye

The apostle Paul had a difficult life. He was beaten, imprisoned, stoned, whipped, slandered, and shipwrecked. Through it all, however, he continued to tell others with joy, hope, and conviction about what Jesus had done. God had called Paul for his purpose. Paul knew God was at work behind the scenes, transforming every circumstance into something that would bring glory to God and good into Paul's own life.

Paul said "we know" with assurance. He did not write "we hope" or "we feel" or even "we pray." God's loving involvement was, and is, an irrefutable fact. When Paul spoke of those people whom God calls for his purpose, Paul was talking about every child who responds to the call of his or her heavenly Father. In the same way that an earthly father cannot show a child something wonderful until the child responds to his call to "come here," God promises to work only wonderful things in the lives of those who follow him.

Paul said "we know" with assurance. He did not write "we hope" or "we feel" or even "we pray."

The good that God worked in Paul's life, and that he vows to work in yours, is not a promise of perfect happiness. It is a promise of eternal purpose. God's plan for you to know him and to spend eternity with him is steadfast. In addition, God will use the pain and the disappointment in your life. He will use them to do something beautiful, to turn heartache into strength and sorrow into joy.

When you are facing difficult circumstances, remember that God is at work transforming everything that happens, both good and bad, into something beneficial for you.

Jesus said, "I leave you peace; my peace I give you. I do not give it to you as the world does. So don't let your hearts be troubled or afraid."

JOHN 14:27 NCV

Jesus' Legacy of Peace

In the Jewish culture, the Hebrew word *shalom* is a customary greeting for both "hello" and "good-bye." *Shalom* means "peace" and so much more. It implies a wish for health, prosperity, and wholeness, as well as a wish for an absence of both internal and external strife.

As Jesus prepared to say good-bye to his closest friends on the night of the Last Supper, he bid them shalom. Jesus's words of farewell were far more than a traditional blessing. They were a gift only the Prince of Peace himself could offer. Jesus offered his followers peace of mind and heart, a peace unlike that of the world they knew, which depended on favorable circumstances. Jesus's offer of peace depended solely on his followers' relationship with him.

These words of Jesus are like his Last Will and Testament. In the same way that a will records how to divide possessions among the survivors of the one who died, John 14:27 is a record of your inheritance. Jesus bequeathed a priceless treasure to all those who fol-

low him, including you. In fact, his gift has set you up for life—both this one and the next. That's because the wholeness found in Jesus's gift of peace is at the heart of true happiness.

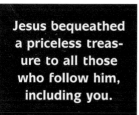

Jesus bequeathed a priceless treasure to all those who follow him, including you.

As you pursue peace by pursuing Jesus, you'll find you are holding the true key to living the good life.

Jesus's gift of peace offers you an alternative to fear and worry, a foretaste of heaven available here and now. As with any inheritance, you have to accept it and use it to enjoy its true benefits.

Though the LORD is supreme, he takes care of those who are humble, but he stays away from the proud.

PSALM 138:6 NCV

The Peril of Pride

In the ancient Middle East, there were many myths about powerful monsters and primeval sea creatures. One Canaanite legend told of a sea monster named Rahab who fought against God's creation of the universe. The word *rahab* is Hebrew for both "acting stormily" and "arrogance." In the same way that the sea creature refused to believe God's power could be greater than its own, arrogant people believe they can succeed in life solely by their own strength.

The bases for human pride are as much a myth as that

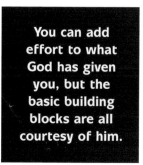

sea creature. Physical abilities, IQ, talents, and accomplishments are all God's gifts. You can add effort to what God has given you, but the basic building blocks are all courtesy of him.

Basing your life on a myth is bad enough. However, the most destructive thing about pride is that it acts like a God-repellent and pushes God away from the center of your life. As God keeps his distance from the proud, his gifts of guidance, wisdom, and comfort move out of reach. While God notices pride right away, you may be unaware of its presence. Ask a close friend if he or she sees evidence of pride in your life. Ask God to help you become more aware of your true motives, and then battle pride with the truth of who God is. The more you come to know and understand him, the more accurate a picture you'll have of yourself—and the more humility will replace pride in your life.

> **You can add effort to what God has given you, but the basic building blocks are all courtesy of him.**

Whenever you feel pride raise its arrogant head in your life, picture the sea monster, Rahab, battling—and losing to—God's supremacy.

I will give you a new heart and put a new spirit within you; I will take the heart of stone out of your flesh and give you a heart of flesh.

EZEKIEL 36:26 NKJV

Heart Transplant

A beating heart is a sign of life. Physically, your heart beats regularly. But spiritually, until you get to know God firsthand, your heart is flat-lining. God promised the prophet Ezekiel (along with everyone who chooses to follow God) the ultimate heart transplant—replacing stone with flesh. This "flesh" is humanity as God originally created it, which is more than simply being human. It is the promise of being fully alive—physically, emotionally, and spiritually—in both this life and the next.

The people of Israel believed a person's "heart" reveals who a person really is. The heart cannot put on airs or be something it is not. It is the emotional and spiritual center of every individual. When God's Spirit becomes the center of people's lives, the Bible says that they are "born again." Along with a new heart comes a new start.

However, this heart transplant is possible only through the power of God's Spirit. Trying to become more loving, generous, and kind through self-effort can never bring a heart of stone to life. Only God's gift of his presence can jump-start a heart into permanent change. God's Spirit at work in you enables you to hear God's voice as he guides your decisions, to see his hand

When God's Spirit becomes the center of people's lives, the Bible says that they are "born again."

as he moves through circumstances, and to fulfill his plans for you to become the person he created you to be.

Through God's words to Ezekiel, you are given a beautiful metaphor to help you understand what happens when God's Spirit comes into your life: you are fully alive for the very first time.

What we have is one body with many parts, each its proper size and in its proper place. No part is important on its own.

1 Corinthians 12:20 msg

Joint Venture

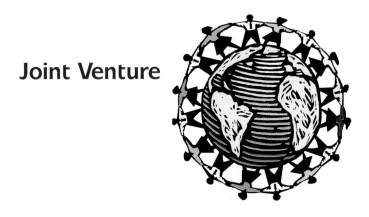

Your body is the perfect picture of how God designed community to work. Every part is interdependent and is vital to the health and strength of the other parts. If your lungs took the day off, your brain would cease to function. If your muscles went on strike, your feet wouldn't be able get you out of bed and off to work.

Paul's picture of the cooperative human body illustrates how every individual is vital to the health of God's church as a whole. It also demonstrates how every part is significant. One part isn't more important than another. You should not regard the person who preaches on Sunday morning as more important than the one who cleans the building before the service. Each individual is necessary. Every gift God gives has a purpose and a place to help fulfill his perfect plan.

Every gift God gives has a purpose and a place to help fulfill his perfect plan.

People often encounter two pitfalls when they evaluate their significance by comparing their gifts with others': (1) they believe their gifts are too small or too big, or (2) they feel that what they do really doesn't matter or that everything would fall apart without them. Paul's words in 1 Corinthians guide you toward the true measure of significance. Though you are of eternal significance to God, your significance on this earth comes solely from what you are a part of—God's body here on earth.

⤳⟋⟋◯

Understanding your significance, and the significance of others, will help you keep a humble, realistic view of yourself. It will also enable you to work more harmoniously in community with others.

All have sinned; all fall short of God's glorious standard. Yet now God in his gracious kindness declares us not guilty. He has done this through Christ Jesus, who has freed us by taking away our sins.

ROMANS 3:23–24 NLT

Missing the Mark

When a person competes in the pole vault, he is focused on doing one thing—jumping higher than the mark where the pole's been set. Once he has jumped, there can be only two outcomes. He either cleared the mark or fell short. If he failed in his attempt to clear the pole, whether he missed by an inch or a foot doesn't matter. He still failed.

The same is true with sin. The Hebrew word for *sin* literally means "to miss the mark." Everyone sins by choosing to go his own way instead of God's way. Some people miss God's mark by an inch; others miss by a mile. How close you come doesn't matter. Close isn't close enough. The moral pole

The good news is that this perfect and faultless God is also perfect and loving.

God has set for you to clear is a high one; it is so high that it's impossible to continually clear it on your own. A perfect, holy God can't embrace anything less than perfect. The good news is that this perfect and faultless God is also perfect and loving. That's why he provided a way for you to clear the bar more consistently, as well as a means for you to avoid a penalty when you miss the mark.

It is important to recognize that everyone sins. Shift your focus to the future, not to the past. Because of Jesus, guilt and the fear of punishment no longer weigh you down. You are free to jump higher than ever before.

When you miss the mark, ask for God's forgiveness, learn from your mistake, and keep moving forward.

I'm eager to encourage you in your faith, but I also want to be encouraged by yours. In this way, each of us will be a blessing to the other.

ROMANS 1:12 NLT

Sharing Your Strength

God is not the only One with the power to bless. You, too, can build others up by showing them special favor, which is what a blessing really is. One way is through the gift of encouragement. Paul expressed his desire to share this valuable gift with other believers who lived in Rome. He'd never met them, and neither had any of the other apostles. But that didn't stop Paul from longing to comfort and strengthen others who shared his faith in God.

Paul's words are a practical example of God's love at work. Love cannot exist in a vacuum. You have to share it. When you encourage others by your loving example, actions, words, or prayers, you'll discover that your gift comes with a bonus. You will, in turn,

> **Love cannot exist in a vacuum. You have to share it.**

be encouraged. In the Greek language, *to encourage* means "to share your strength with others" as well as "to be mutually comforted." The more you take the opportunity to cheer on and support those around you, the more you'll experience the joy that love can bring.

God has used Paul's words and the example of his life to strengthen and inspire people for more than two thousand years. You never know when a simple word of encouragement to a friend or even a stranger will cause a ripple effect that will be felt throughout eternity. Put the principle behind Paul's words to the test today. God can turn your simple gift of encouragement into a tremendous blessing.

Be encouraged, and act on what you've learned. Strengthen others by sharing how much they mean to you and to God.

You must worship no other gods, but only the LORD, for he is a God who is passionate about his relationship with you.

EXODUS 34:14 NLT

The One and Only

The Israelites saw God part the Red Sea and save them from captivity in Egypt. But soon afterward, they gave up on the God who'd rescued them. They chose to worship a golden calf instead. When Moses returned from receiving the Ten Commandments, he saw the Israelites—God's people—engaged in idolatry. Moses threw the tablets to the ground, shattering them just as the people had shattered God's first commandment—to worship only God.

God is a God of second chances, however. God gave Moses new tablets and reiterated his commands. Those

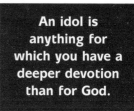

commands are as important today as they were for the Israelites, because God designed his commands to build relationship with him and with the people around you. Obeying God's commands helps you to love well.

The first commandment, that God alone is to be worshiped, is at the heart of them all. God doesn't ask you for worship because his ego needs stroking. He asks it because worshiping him alone is the best thing that could happen to you. You don't have to kneel before a golden calf to worship idols. An idol is anything for which you have a deeper devotion than for God. An idol could be power, money,

> **An idol is anything for which you have a deeper devotion than for God.**

comfort, pleasure, even religion. Worshiping God above everything else keeps life in the proper perspective. God is passionate about his relationship with you. Worshiping him alone helps you become more passionate about him.

Consider what's important in your life. Weigh your relationship with God in light of everything else. Ask God to help you identify anything that you give higher priority to than getting to know him better.

The Word became a human and lived among us. We saw his glory—the glory that belongs to the only Son of the Father—and he was full of grace and truth.

JOHN 1:14 NCV

Special Delivery

The day God came to earth is much more than a sweet tale on which to base a holiday. It is a miracle of dynamic proportions, and John tells the wonder of it all. God himself came to live on earth. That is the heart of the Christmas story. The God of the universe made his home here on earth so that people could better understand him, connect with him, and experience his kindness. The Word is God's most intimate, and informative, communication with those whom he created.

It is interesting that such a pivotal verse about Jesus does not even contain his name. That's because *Word* was a powerful symbol in both Greek philosophy and Jewish tradition. The Greeks referred to *logos* or *Word* as the creative force that brought the world

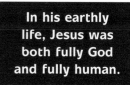

In his earthly life, Jesus was both fully God and fully human.

into being. Everyone at that time understood that referring to Jesus as the Word was the same as calling him the eternal Creator.

If you're going to believe in this eternal Creator, you need to understand who he is. The biggest mistake people make about Jesus is to minimize either his deity or his humanity. In his earthly life, Jesus was both fully God and fully human. John emphasized this point throughout his entire Gospel. Although both the Old and New Testaments are filled with important verses about Jesus, John 1:14 clearly states who Jesus is and what he wants to impart to you.

Jesus's humanity enabled him to relate to your human problems, while his divinity gave him the power to help you overcome them.

God's word is alive and working and is sharper than a double-edged sword. It cuts all the way into us, where the soul and the spirit are joined, to the center of our joints and bones. And it judges the thoughts and feelings in our hearts.

Hebrews 4:12 NCV

Blade of Truth

The Bible is not your ordinary book. Like a surgeon's scalpel, it has the power to slice through lies to expose raw truth. It can prick a guilty conscience, heal a broken heart, or open eyes that have long been blind to God's existence. The verse in Hebrews is like the Bible's warning label. It lets you know that what you're holding in your hands should be handled carefully—and that it will leave a reader or listener a changed person.

That's because the Bible is much more than merely print on paper. The Bible is alive with the power of God's Spirit. Like Jesus, its genesis is both fully human and fully divine. Though ordinary people wrote it, God worked through those writers in an extraordinary way. Throughout the Bible's sixty-six books of history, prophecy, and guidelines for living written over a period of six hundred years by more than thirty authors using three languages, there is a consistency of purpose about God and his plan that mere coincidence could never achieve.

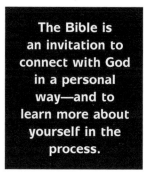

The Bible is an invitation to connect with God in a personal way—and to learn more about yourself in the process.

The Bible is not a reference book to teach you about God. The Bible is an invitation to connect with God in a personal way—and to learn more about yourself in the process. The more time you spend reading the Bible and meditating on how God wants you to apply what you've read, the more you'll learn to recognize the whisper of God's Spirit in your life and to see his hand at work in the world around you.

Get to know God better by becoming better acquainted with the Bible. Reading one psalm and a chapter from one of the Gospels each morning is a great way to begin.

I will give you a new
heart and put a new spirit
within you; I will take the
heart of stone out of your
flesh and give you a heart
of flesh.

Ezekiel 36:26 NKJV

You should pray like this: "Our Father in heaven, may your name always be kept holy. May your kingdom come and what you want be done, here on earth as it is in heaven. Give us the food we need for each day. Forgive us for our sins, just as we have forgiven those who sinned against us. And do not cause us to be tempted, but save us from the Evil One."

MATTHEW 6:9–13 NCV

Praying Like Jesus

These verses are some of the most-often-repeated words in the Bible. Various Bible translations differ on a word here or there, but the heart of the Lord's Prayer remains the same. Right before Jesus shared how to pray, he emphasized how not to pray. One of the things he said not to do was repeat the same words over and over again without thinking about what is being said. That's exactly what many people do with the Lord's Prayer.

Use the Lord's Prayer the way Jesus intended. Let it help you better understand, and put into practice, three vital elements of prayer: praise, petition, and confession. Jesus's prayer began with thanks for who God is, a Father deserving honor. Then Jesus requested help by sharing personal needs, both physical and spiritual. He asked for the basic provision of food, as well as for the protection and the strength necessary to do what God 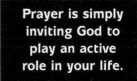 wanted. He also prayed for the needs of others, asking that their lives would align more with God's desires.

Jesus had nothing to confess, but he knew those listening did, so he modeled how to ask for forgiveness. Confessing where you've failed keeps communication with God honest and open and helps you become more merciful to those who fail you. As Jesus demonstrated, prayer is simply inviting God to play an active role in your life.

The Lord's Prayer is Jesus's most concrete lesson on prayer. Pray as Jesus did. Share your deepest concerns with God, and invite God to make your heart and your will more like his.

Prayer is simply inviting God to play an active role in your life.

Jesus said, "The thief does not come except to steal, and to kill, and to destroy. I have come that they may have life, and that they may have it more abundantly."

JOHN 10:10 NKJV

Living Life to the Fullest

Jesus often used parables and metaphors to help people get a better picture of the principles and truths he was talking about. He referred to himself as things like a vine, a lamb, or a bridegroom. He also described himself as the Good Shepherd. He wanted his followers to understand the difference between how a good shepherd cares and sacrifices for the benefit of his sheep, while thieves and hired hands use sheep only to benefit themselves. Jesus wanted them to know he was a leader who always had his followers' best interests at heart.

Jesus proclaimed the end result of this tender care for his sheep, which makes the verse one of the most important verses in the Bible. It is Jesus's statement of purpose; it is his promise to those who follow him. That includes you. What Jesus promised is life. Not just ordinary, breathing-in-and-out, making-it-by-the-seat-of-your-pants life, but an authentic, eternal, hang-on-to-your-seats-because-another-miracle's-coming abundant life.

> The kind of abundance that Jesus promised is a measure of the quality of life, not the quantity of possessions.

The kind of abundance that Jesus promised is a measure of the quality of life, not the quantity of possessions. You can't measure this abundance in square footage or bottom lines. Jesus promised to provide a surplus of what makes life worth living—things like love, grace, guidance, forgiveness, and joy. These are Jesus's gifts to you, a life that is overflowing with riches of the heart that no one can ever take away.

⸰⸰⸰

Keeping in mind Jesus's promise to you of an abundant life gives you reason for constant hope and thanks. It also fosters contentment by helping you find joy in the abundance of what matters most.

God is our refuge and strength, a very present help in trouble. Therefore we will not fear, even though the earth be removed, and though the mountains be carried into the midst of the sea . . . "Be still, and know that I am God."

PSALM 46:1–2, 10 NKJV

Stop, Look, Listen, and Trust

The Psalms are a tapestry of human emotions. The poetry of prayer weaves together anger, fear, joy, longing, despair, praise, and passion. These verses sum up God's response to those prayers. Their truth is the thread of peace and comfort that runs through the entire book of Psalms, as well as the rest of the Bible — and the life of every individual who walks with God. God's answer to those who are emotionally troubled is brief and straightforward: stop and remember who is on your side.

Psalm 46 talks about earthquakes felling mountains, cities being destroyed, nations being in an uproar, kingdoms crumbling. It talks about the final destruction of the world itself. The overall tone of the psalm is anything but quiet and still. One sentence, however, says to "be still," and the focal point of emotion changes from outside chaos to internal rest.

That's why this psalm was written as a song. It proclaimed a message everyone needed to hear.

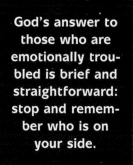

God's answer to those who are emotionally troubled is brief and straightforward: stop and remember who is on your side.

Let the truth of these verses find a home in your heart today. When life gets busy or chaotic, it's easy to get distracted. You wind up focusing on problems instead of the One who holds the answer to your problems in his hands. When that happens, stop. Focus on who God is and how much he loves you. Share your own heartfelt psalm of prayer with the God of power and compassion. Be still and know God is near.

The words in Psalm 46 hold incredible power when it comes to knowing God is near in any and every situation. Memorize them. Meditate on them. Keep them close at heart for when you need them most.

In all the work you are doing, work the best you can. Work as if you were doing it for the Lord, not for people.

COLOSSIANS 3:23 NCV

Job Description: Excellence

Work is a noble calling. God commends people for doing it well, and he also does work himself. When God created the world, he worked. The excellence of his work is evident in everything he made. He even took a day off to review the results of his efforts and declared them "good." God continues to work, sustaining what he created that very first week in the world's history.

Since God created you in his image, work should be a part of your life. Doing it well reflects God's creativity and character. It is easy, however, to lose your motivation when a job is difficult or you become bored with doing the same thing day after day. Paul's words to the Colossians can help you keep your work in its proper perspective. Working the best you can literally means working "out from the soul." You are not working simply to pay the bills, please your boss, or pass the time of day. God set this job in front of you. When you do your job well, God notices, even if no one else does.

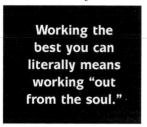

Working the best you can literally means working "out from the soul."

This section of Colossians was originally directed toward slaves. It encouraged them to remain positive and productive, even if they were working in bondage under a tyrant. If a slave, who could be beaten even if he did a job well, could strive for excellence by maintaining a Colossians 3:23 perspective, certainly it is something you can do in whatever job is facing you.

Focus on God's perspective throughout the day and imagine at all times that he is your boss.

May God himself, the God who makes everything holy and whole, make you holy and whole, put you together—spirit, soul, and body—and keep you fit for the coming of our Master, Jesus Christ.

1 Thessalonians 5:23 msg

Piecing Life Together

A jigsaw puzzle is made up of multiple parts. It is only when these parts are put together, when the puzzle is whole and complete, that you see the picture it was designed to display. Your life is the same way. Your life is made up of many complex components: family life, job, hobbies, physical health, emotional state, present circumstances, past experiences, hopes for the future, relationship with God. It would be easy to feel that your life is fragmented, like unconnected pieces of a puzzle that don't seem to fit. But that isn't the way you were designed.

God designed you to be whole and complete, where every part of your life interconnects with his love and his plan. This doesn't happen automatically or overnight. That is why the apostle Paul asked God to help the people in the church at Thessalonica to continue to move closer toward wholeness in their lives.

> **God designed you to be whole and complete, where every part of your life interconnects with his love and his plan.**

He recognized that people cannot achieve the process of maturity that leads to wholeness through self-effort. It requires the power of God. Paul's prayer is one you need to pray for yourself.

Ask God to help pull the pieces of your life together according to his original design. As you choose to keep God at the center of your life, you'll find your own unique "picture" becoming more complete. Your job, your relationships, and your dreams work together, linked to one another because they are each solidly linked back to God.

Let Paul's prayer make you more aware of the big picture behind what's going on in your life. Ask God to help you get a better glimpse of what that really is.

See how the farmer waits for the precious fruit of the earth, waiting patiently for it until it receives the early and latter rain. You also be patient. Establish your hearts, for the coming of the Lord is at hand.

JAMES 5:7–8 NKJV

Watching and Waiting

God's timing is always perfect. He parted the Red Sea when his people needed it most—when they were trapped between the rushing waters and an approaching army. God allowed the water to flow again, but only after Moses and the Israelites had made it safely across. God provided what the people needed at the precise moment that it would make the greatest difference.

From a human vantage point, it isn't always easy to recognize that opportune moment. Waiting for God's answer, when your own internal timer has already gone off, can make you feel as if God isn't listening or he simply doesn't care.

When you find yourself in that situation, take a lesson from this important verse in James and put yourself in a farmer's shoes. You can't rush a perfect harvest or an answer to prayer. As

God will answer your prayers when the time is right.

a farmer waits for the fruit of his labor, he doesn't just sit around complaining about how long the growing season is. He continues to work. He trusts God, and his patience grows right along with his fruit.

James provides a valuable tip for those who wait. He advises you to *establish* your heart, which means "to firmly plant your life and expectations in the fertile soil of God's truth." There is a bountiful harvest as certain as the fulfillment of God's promises: the Lord will return; the hard times you face will end; and God will answer your prayers when the time is right.

The image of a patient farmer is an encouraging visual picture for prayer. Picture every prayer as a seed planted in God's will. As you wait, picture them ripening, trusting in God's perfect harvesttime.

If Christ is not risen, your faith is futile; you are still in your sins!

1 CORINTHIANS 15:17 NKJV

Empty Tombs

The moment Jesus rose from the dead, everything changed. How God related to people in the Old Testament (by speaking to the whole nation through prophets) gave way to the New (by speaking to people individually through his Spirit). God forgave the sins of those who chose to follow him. Death was defeated. Eternal life was certain. There was absolute proof Jesus was who he said he was, God and Savior.

The apostle Paul's words to the Corinthian church remove the option of believing the Bible is a collection of morality myths. His words do not allow for Jesus to be regarded as a prophet or a good teacher. Either Jesus rose from the dead, proving he was who he said he was and that he did what he said he would do, or your faith is useless. Paul, the writer of 1 and 2 Corinthians, went on to say that if Jesus did not rise from the dead, then Christians are to be pitied as the most miserable people on earth because they base their faith, their hope, and their purpose in life on a lie.

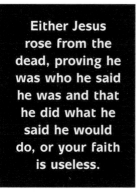

Either Jesus rose from the dead, proving he was who he said he was and that he did what he said he would do, or your faith is useless.

History says otherwise, however. More than five hundred witnesses saw Jesus alive after he died on the cross. The bodies of other great religious leaders, such as Buddha and Mohammed, remain dead in their graves. Only Jesus lives beyond the grave. This important verse is a subtle reminder that because of Jesus, one day you will too.

Though Jesus's death paid the price for people's transgressions, Jesus's resurrection is evidence of God's acceptance of that payment. Let Paul's words help keep you grounded in the historical facts that support your faith.

You should know that your body is a temple for the Holy Spirit who is in you. You have received the Holy Spirit from God. So you do not belong to yourselves, because you were bought by God for a price. So honor God with your bodies.

1 CORINTHIANS 6:19–20 NCV

God's Dwelling Place

In Paul's day, the city of Corinth was infamous for sexual debauchery and decadence. There was even a slang Greek verb that meant "to act like a Corinthian," which implied that one took part in sexual immorality. The church of Corinth, though filled with true believers in Jesus, continued to struggle with the sinful excesses of its culture. In response to the church's repeated failure to set itself apart for God instead of blending into Corinthian society, Paul directed his comments in a letter to this struggling church. His words today, as well as then, are a good heart-and-body check for every believer.

Thanks to Jesus's sacrifice, your body is now God's home. In the Old Testament, God's presence stayed physically close to his people by dwelling in an elaborate temple complex. God dictated every detail of the temple's construction, as well as strict rules on how to keep it holy and fit for his use. God's Spirit dwelled in an especially sacred part of the temple called the Holy of Holies. In Greek, this place was called *naos*. Paul used that same word here. Your body is God's Holy of Holies.

> **Thanks to Jesus's sacrifice, your body is now God's home.**

When a guest comes to your home, you honor that guest by putting things in order and doing all you can to make that person feel comfortable. By taking care of yourself physically and steering clear of sexual sin, you are doing the same for God. You are giving your heavenly Father a warm welcome home.

⁓⫯〇

Your body is a sacred place where God's Spirit dwells. How you treat yourself physically is a reflection of the kind of dwelling place you desire to offer the Father, who loves you.

It is not fancy hair, gold jewelry, or fine clothes that should make you beautiful. No, your beauty should come from within you—the beauty of a gentle and quiet spirit that will never be destroyed and is very precious to God.

1 PETER 3:3–4 NCV

Inside Story

The women of ancient Rome were much like many women today. They worked hard to be beautiful. Elaborate hairstyles made up of tiny knots plaited with gold and jewels and then piled high on the head were all the rage. One drawback was that fashionable Roman women feared going to sleep lest they muss their hairdos. But those women wholeheartedly believed that their passion for fashion was worth the extra effort, because beauty was what was going to keep their husbands faithful, satisfied with them alone.

Fashion trends today tend toward plastic surgery, excessive dieting, and a closet full of haute couture. Women's (and even men's) motivations haven't changed much in two thousand years. People strive to look beautiful so that others will perceive them as valuable and desirable. The apostle Peter

True lasting beauty is found in a heart that rests secure in God's love.

directed his readers to refocus from external beauty to internal beauty. From what fades to what is eternal. From what pleases men to what pleases God.

True lasting beauty is found in a heart that rests secure in God's love. That gentle and quiet spirit doesn't need to strive for attention. It is adorned with spiritual instead of physical riches. Authentic inner beauty, and not artificial glamour, attracts others to what is truly valuable — the unique person whom God holds precious in his sight.

~))(©

Peter's words are not a call to dowdiness. They are merely a reminder to keep your priorities straight when it comes to becoming a beautiful person. Concentrate on what matters most — the inside, not the outside.

Do not worry about anything, but pray and ask God for everything you need, always giving thanks. And God's peace, which is so great we cannot understand it, will keep your hearts and minds in Christ Jesus.

PHILIPPIANS 4:6–7 NCV

Panic Attack

Worry is a stealthy, yet formidable, enemy. Worry can creep into your life quietly, masquerading as an acceptable human response to living in an imperfect world. But worry is neither acceptable nor harmless. Worry is a dangerous diversion that leads you to focus on your problems instead of on God, who loves you and is in control. There is an easy, effective way to eliminate worry — pray.

Praying about both the big and small things in your life is a way of constantly realigning your point of view with

God's perspective. Prayer is more than simply asking God for help. It is also a time of worship and thanks. Thanking God for his past help and blessings is a gift to yourself, as well as to God. Every thank-you serves as a personal reminder of God's love and faithfulness in your life, and it provides you

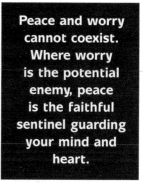

Peace and worry cannot coexist. Where worry is the potential enemy, peace is the faithful sentinel guarding your mind and heart.

with a source of comfort, strength, encouragement, and peace.

Peace and worry cannot coexist. Where worry is the potential enemy, peace is the faithful sentinel guarding your mind and heart. There is nothing passive about the word *guard*. It's a Greek military term that paints a picture of a stronghold being protected by a vigilant garrison of watchmen. When you allow prayer to defeat worry in your life, God's peace will be your watchman through any and every situation.

At the first sign of worry, practice the life-changing principle found in Philippians 4:6–7. Tell God what you're anxious about. Thank him for who he is, for what he has done, and for the peace he provides.

This day I call heaven and earth as witnesses against you that I have set before you life and death, blessings and curses. Now choose life.

DEUTERONOMY 30:19 NIV

Life-or-Death Decisions

After forty years of wandering through the desert, the Jordan River was all that stood between the people of Israel and the Promised Land. Most of the generation Moses called together to speak to on that day had never known the Egyptian captivity of their parents. Their home had been the desert, and their hope had been the land across the Jordan. From where the Israelites stood, it looked like the hard times were finally over. Stability and prosperity lay ahead.

Yet Moses knew that even in a land of promise and plenty, every individual had a choice. The choice Moses shared with the people of Israel is the same choice God gives every individual today. You can make a choice to follow God and receive the benefits of an obedient life. Or you can make a choice that dishonors God and reap the natural negative consequences of your actions.

Although crucial to determining your eternal destiny, accepting or rejecting God's gift of salvation is only one choice you make in this life. Every minute is filled with choices, choices that draw you closer to God or farther away from him. Choosing life means choosing God. When you choose life, you prevent curses

Every minute is filled with choices, choices that draw you closer to God or farther away from him.

(which are simply the opposite of blessings) from taking hold. Moses's words are a reminder that your choices, both big and small, matter. Choose wisely. Choose life.

God's grace gives you the freedom to choose between good and evil. God's love allows consequences to act as a guide, helping you make decisions that honor God while improving the quality of your life.

By grace you have been saved through faith, and that not of yourselves; it is the gift of God, not of works, lest anyone should boast.

EPHESIANS 2:8–9 NKJV

Gift of Life

Grace sets Christianity apart from every other religion in the world. *Charis*, the Greek word for *grace*, literally means "free gift." That's what God promises, a gift of eternal life with no strings attached, one that you can't receive any other way than through the unmerited generosity of the Giver. You can't gain eternal life through good works or lose it through bad. Faith in Jesus is the only channel through which you can receive this priceless gift.

Yet God was extending grace long before Jesus came to earth. It began in the Garden of Eden. When Adam and Eve chose to turn away from God, he allowed them to suffer the conse- quences of their actions, but the depth of his love for those he had created would not let that be the final word.

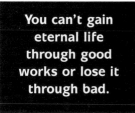

You can't gain eternal life through good works or lose it through bad.

He extended the free gift of grace by promising to send Someone who could redeem, or pay for, what had been done. He fulfilled that promise through Jesus.

Good works are evidence of a growing faith in God and demonstrate the power of God's grace to transform a life. Good works bring honor to God, blessings to others, and joy to the one who performs them. But they have no power to open the doors of heaven. Remembering this truth will turn any urge to brag into an occasion for praise.

When comparing Christianity with other religions, focus on God's grace. Explaining God's free gift to you will help oth- ers understand you don't put yourself "above" them. Everyone's imperfect and therefore in need of God's grace.

In all the work you are doing, work the best you can. Work as if you were doing it for the Lord, not for people.

COLOSSIANS 3:23 NCV

The only temptation that has come to you is that which everyone has. But you can trust God, who will not permit you to be tempted more than you can stand. But when you are tempted, he will also give you a way to escape so that you will be able to stand it.

1 CORINTHIANS 10:13 NCV

Escape Route

Many verses in the Bible ask you to do things that sound impossible. Love your enemies. Deal with your anger before the day ends. Give generously, even to strangers. Don't regard the opposite sex with lust in your heart. Forgive those who've hurt you. A common response may be, "Nice sentiment, but this is the real world. You don't know what I'm up against." It is true the world is filled with temptations, enticements to take a self-centered approach toward

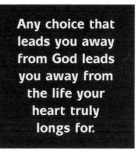

pleasure and personal gain. But appearances are deceiving. Any choice that leads you away from God leads you away from the life your heart truly longs for.

Trusting God is the antidote for making bad choices in life. You are not alone in your struggle. Everyone faces pressure, both internal and external, to make choices that dishonor God. Even Jesus was tempted in the same ways you are. Yet Jesus put into practice the truth promised here. God faithfully provided an escape route from temptation, and Jesus took it.

> **Any choice that leads you away from God leads you away from the life your heart truly longs for.**

You have the same opportunity for victory. Be on the lookout for God's escape route when temptations come your way. Your escape may come through the power of prayer, accountability with others, or avoiding situations that lead you away from God instead of toward him. Whatever the escape route, God has promised that you will have the ability to make the right choice.

Memorizing this verse in 1 Corinthians is a great way to become more aware of the temptations you face and of the God-given options you have to avoid surrendering to them.

Jesus said, "Come to Me, all you who labor and are heavy laden, and I will give you rest. Take My yoke upon you and learn from Me, for I am gentle and lowly in heart, and you will find rest for your souls."

MATTHEW 11:28–29 NKJV

Sharing the Load

When Jesus spoke to people, he often used parables and word pictures that incorporated familiar everyday situations so his listeners could better identify with the spiritual principles he wanted to share. Jesus spoke about finding rest through being "yoked" to him.

In Jesus's day, a yoke had two distinct meanings. The first was the wooden harness used to link oxen together to plow a field. The second was a slang term referring to Jewish laws and traditions. It was said that Jews were "yoked" to the Torah. In other words, they were burdened by carrying around the Old Testament commands as well as the numerous additional laws dictated by the Pharisees. Trying to follow that many rules would be exhausting for anyone. Jesus let it be known that relationship, not rule-following, is the key to obedience. Walking closely with God through prayer and allowing his Spirit and his Word to guide you take you from the burden of legalism to the freedom of a righteous life.

> **The rest Jesus offers is a quiet strength and companionship that helps you continue moving forward without burning out physically, mentally, or emotionally.**

The rest Jesus offers isn't an escape from work and struggle. The rest Jesus offers is a quiet strength and companionship that helps you continue moving forward without burning out physically, mentally, or emotionally. All you need to do is "come," "take," and "learn." Learning how to rest in God when times are hard is a process, but walking side by side with the world's greatest Teacher sharing your load is a journey that leads to joy.

When times are difficult, picture Jesus walking alongside you as a reminder that you're not alone. Speak to him honestly about the help you need and your thankfulness for the help he has already provided.

$\mathbf{D}$o not be conformed to this world, but be transformed by the renewing of your mind, that you may prove what is that good and acceptable and perfect will of God.

ROMANS 12:2 NKJV

Time to Change Your Mind

Your mind is like the control center of your body. It helps direct your thoughts, your actions, and your emotions. Before God's Spirit made his home inside you, you ran that control center the way you thought was best. Chances are, the culture and practices of those around you helped shape your thoughts and consequently your actions. But once you invited God's Spirit into your life, there was a change in influence, leadership, and direction.

Choosing to renew your mind is the key to making that change complete. God guides and directs your mind, but he does not control it. God provides you with the power to transform your mind, to change the way you think so that your mind is more in line with his heart—to allow your mind to become all he originally designed it to be.

The Greek word for *conform* actually translates as "masquerade." Without God in your life, you live a charade and are not your authentic self. God's transformation of who you once pretended to be into who he created you to be is an ongoing process. Part of this process is testing what you believe by putting your faith into practice. Experiments help prove scientific truths. Living what you believe helps prove spiritual

Without God in your life, you live a charade and are not your authentic self.

truths. As you practice what you have learned about changing the way you think, you will better understand who you are and what God's desire is for your life.

You can help renew your mind by providing an environment that's favorable to the process. Carefully choose what you watch, take part in, and listen to, making sure that your choices line up with what pleases God.

Blessed be the God and Father of our Lord Jesus Christ, the Father of mercies and God of all comfort, who comforts us in all our tribulation, that we may be able to comfort those who are in any trouble, with the comfort with which we ourselves are comforted by God.

2 CORINTHIANS 1:3–4 NKJV

Consolation Prize

The apostle Paul began his second letter to the church in Corinth just as he did his other letters, with a brief introduction that leads straight into thanksgiving. Paul's cause for thanks, however, sets this letter apart. You can be thankful for comfort only if you've known the pain of suffering. Paul certainly did, and so did his Corinthian audience. So does every individual who reads these words today.

Though levels of personal suffering differ, pain and heartache are universal. Yet amid that sobering truth, Paul gave reason for praise. God's comfort is at hand in every type of trouble. The original meaning of the old-fashioned-sounding word *tribulation* covers a lot of ground. It can mean "distress," "affliction," "persecution," or simply "great misery." God's comfort fits any and every situation perfectly.

Through Paul, God provided even more good news: there is a positive, productive side to suffering. As God comforts you, you learn how to better comfort others. This is different from simply being sympathetic toward people and their problems. The Greek word for *comfort* implies action. It means "to come alongside and help." God actively comes alongside you with strength, encouragement, hope, and healing, and you gain the ability to

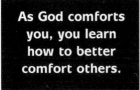

As God comforts you, you learn how to better comfort others.

do the same for others. When you are struggling with difficulty in your life, remember to reach out to God and then to others. God provides comfort to help you become a comforter like him.

When you're facing tough times, follow Paul's example. Praise God for the comfort he's already promised, and then ask him to help you use your own experience to bring comfort to someone else.

Whoever does not care for his own relatives, especially his own family members, has turned against the faith and is worse than someone who does not believe in God.

1 TIMOTHY 5:8 NCV

All in the Family

Paul gave advice to the young pastor Timothy on how to help organize and maintain a vital, God-honoring church. One area Paul discussed was meeting the needs of others. It seems that some members of the congregation were giving their time, energy, and resources to the church but neglecting the needs of their own families. Paul addressed this problem to help the people at Ephesus set their priorities straight.

The truth behind his words can help do the same for you. Paul's warning is clear-cut and to the point: anyone who turns his back on his own family turns his back on God. It's true that in biblical times, there were no government-run social programs to help widows, orphans, and women who had been left impoverished after their husbands divorced them. Today, people in similar situations have places to turn for help. But that doesn't alleviate the

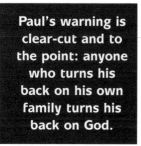

Paul's warning is clear-cut and to the point: anyone who turns his back on his own family turns his back on God.

responsibility God gives each person in providing for those in his or her own family.

Providing entails more than financial responsibility. Supporting your parents, spouse, and children emotionally is equally important. When God previously commanded his children to love one another, he obviously meant that to include their own family circle. Use Paul's words as a reminder to regularly ask for God's guidance in knowing how to care for the people whom he has placed closest to you. Use Paul's words to better meet apparent needs as well as needs that aren't so apparent.

Loving one another and caring for your family are joyous and rewarding commands from God, and he will give you guidance to do both.

Submit to God. Resist the devil and he will flee from you.

JAMES 4:7 NKJV

Battle Plan

The devil is referred to by many names throughout the Bible—accuser, tempter, deceiver, slanderer, enemy, Satan. One thing the Bible never calls him is a mythical creature. He is as real as God himself. There's no point in resisting someone who isn't there.

You need to know more, however, than that Satan exists. You need to know exactly what to do to defeat Satan. On the same day you aligned yourself with God, you gained this "adversary," which is what the word *Satan* literally means. Satan has no personal interest in you. His only aim

is to hurt God. One way he tries to do that is by trying to hurt the ones whom God loves. Satan is only a prideful, fallen angel. He isn't all-knowing or all-powerful. Yet he can still wreak havoc, causing you to doubt God's love or tempting you to go down the wrong road.

But you can stop Satan in his tracks. First, submit to God. In the original language, *submit* is a military command that means "to get into your proper rank." That's accomplished by humbly putting every aspect of your life under God's loving authority. Only then are you prepared to defeat the devil. *Resist* is also a military command that means "to stand bravely against." Stand against your adversary by recalling biblical truths. Strengthen your resolve through prayer. Turn your back on anything that entices you to turn away from God. Satan will flee from the battle before it has even begun.

Satan is only a prideful, fallen angel.

Satan has no future. Jesus assured Satan's ultimate defeat by dying on the cross. The potential skirmishes that James alludes to are nothing more than diversionary tactics from an opponent who is destined to lose.

Christ is the mediator of the new covenant, that those who are called may receive the promised eternal inheritance—now that he has died as a ransom to set them free from the sins committed under the first covenant.

HEBREWS 9:15 NIV

Eternal Will and Testament

Words like *mediator, covenant,* and *inheritance* in the book of Hebrews give the impression of a legal document. Actually, the entire book of Hebrews differs in writing style from the rest of the letters in the New Testament. Its unknown author presents a thesis-like case, methodically stating why faith in Jesus is a logical and God-designed spiritual progression from Judaism.

The verse at the heart of what the author wanted his readers to understand proclaims that Jesus is both a *mediator,* "someone who makes peace between two parties," and a *testator,* "someone who determines the conditions and bene-

fits of the inheritance he leaves behind." The words *testament* and *covenant* are interchangeable. The Old Testament and the New Testament could just as easily be called the Old Covenant and the New Covenant, since the two parts of the Bible really focus on covenant. Under the Old Covenant, or Old Testament, God accepted the sacrifice of animals

> **Jesus saved your life by substituting his own in payment for every wrong you've ever done and ever will do.**

as a way to cover up the wrongs people had done. Under the New Covenant, the wrongs were permanently erased by a different kind of sacrifice — Jesus's gift of his own life.

A last will and testament is valid only after someone dies, and then it is irrevocable. That means Jesus's death guaranteed your inheritance. Jesus saved your life by substituting his own in payment for every wrong you've ever done and ever will do. Because of this, you will receive what you never could have earned on your own — the ultimate freedom of living a life that never ends.

~~~

Jesus's testament to you is not only a guarantee, but it is also a true source of encouragement. When God makes a promise, it's like a legal document. He will fulfill every word.

From the time the world was created, people have seen the earth and sky and all that God made. They can clearly see his invisible qualities—his eternal power and divine nature. So they have no excuse whatsoever for not knowing God.

Romans 1:20 nlt

The Gospel of Creation

The Milky Way, the Great Barrier Reef, the northern lights, the miracle of birth . . . the universe is filled with wonders that humans cannot replicate on their own, wonders that point to the existence of Someone as Creator. People disagree over who this Creator is and whether he is actively involved in the world today. Yet the intricacy, orderliness, and sheer awesomeness of the natural world confirm what the human heart has felt since the dawn of time—there is more to this life than meets the eye.

What is visible proclaims the existence of something invisible. Some people have rejected this truth, but that doesn't make it any less true. Paul discussed in his letter to the Romans how people knew God was there but did not thank him or

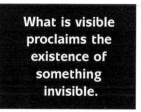

What is visible proclaims the existence of something invisible.

give glory to him for what he'd done. They chose instead to go their own foolish ways. The good news is that God is real. His fingerprints are everywhere, and you can understand more about who he is by simply studying what he's made.

Knowing about God's character is not the same thing as knowing him. However, recognizing there is a God is the first step in seeking him. Through the wonder of creation, God has left no room for anyone's choosing to do anything less.

You can make the truth found in Romans more real to you by exploring the world around you, thereby discovering new things about God's character. Praise God for everything you learn.

In your lives you must think and act like Christ Jesus.

PHILIPPIANS 2:5 NCV

A Servant's Heart

Modern culture encourages individuals to fight for their rights, push their way to the top, and always look out for number one. Jesus demonstrated a different way to approach life, with the attitude of a servant who lays aside his rights for the benefit of others. In his letter to the church at Philippi, Paul challenged the Philippians to make a countercultural choice and to follow Jesus's example.

To understand what it means to have the attitude and actions of Jesus alive and working within you, read the Gospels. Note how Jesus treated people. Note his patience, his compassion, and his sacrificial perspective on life. He voluntarily put earthly limitations on his heavenly form in order to bless others. He continually asked his Father for "thy will," not "my will," to be accomplished. Out of anyone who ever lived on this earth, Jesus had more reason

> **Your attitude influences your decisions and actions and, ultimately, the effect they have on the lives of others.**

to demand that others put him on a pedestal than anyone else. He deserved to be honored and served. Instead, out of an attitude of humility, he chose to be the servant of all.

Your attitude influences your decisions and actions and, ultimately, the effect they have on the lives of others. A selfish, self-centered attitude will eventually lead to self-destruction. A humble, God-centered attitude will lead to deeper personal peace and a greater positive impact on the world around you. It also will bring joy and honor to God, who dearly loves you. Help keep your attitude in check by keeping this in mind.

Love is the motivation behind the attitude that you are asked to emulate. The closer you draw to God, the deeper your love will grow and the more like Jesus your attitude will become.

God be merciful to us and bless us, and cause His face to shine upon us, that Your way may be known on earth, Your salvation among all nations.

Psalm 67:1–2 NKJV

Message to the Masses

The Bible is filled with examples of how God blesses his people. In the Old Testament, God's blessings were typically physical ones, expressed in the form of personal provision, protection, and prosperity. In the New Testament, God's Spirit promised even richer blessings, such as peace, comfort, joy, hope, and eternal life—not to mention God's greatest blessing of all, the gift of his Son.

Like any loving father, God blesses his children simply because he loves them and delights in giving them pleasure.

However, Psalm 67 reveals an even greater purpose behind God's gifts: God's blessings can provide the world with tangible evidence that he is active, involved, and graciously good.

One lesson this psalm teaches is that there is nothing wrong with asking God for his blessings. It also gives an Old Testament glimpse into God's New Testament plans. In the Old Testament, God primarily blessed the one distinct group of people he chose to demonstrate his love to and through—the people of Israel. Yet even then, God loved all the nations of the earth and wanted them also to experience his blessing of salvation. As the Israelites drew closer to God, their desires better reflected God's own. The same can be true for you. As God's love for the world fills your heart and your prayers, ask him to use every blessing he bestows on you to provide others with a clearer picture of who he is.

> God's blessings can provide the world with tangible evidence that he is active, involved, and graciously good.

Consider the fact that every blessing can be a tool. Ask God to help you use your blessings wisely, in ways that draw others closer to him.

The LORD says, "Do not remember the for-
mer things, nor consider the things of old.
Behold, I will do a new thing, now it shall
spring forth; shall you not know it?"

ISAIAH 43:18–19 NKJV

Moving On

The people of Israel made plenty of mistakes and suffered generations of consequences. They'd been slaves in
Egypt, wandered the desert for forty years, and were
presently at war with Assyria. Because of repeatedly dis-
obeying and distancing themselves from God, they'd lived
with crippling fear, enemy invasions, and backbreaking
bondage off and on for centuries. Along with words of
rebuke and warning, the prophet Isaiah offered those des-
perate people words of hope, which summed up the heart of
his message.

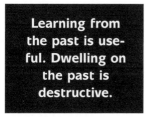

Through Isaiah, God promised his people he was doing something fresh and innovative. The Hebrew word for *new* conveys both expectancy and optimism. It describes something "unprecedented in its wonderful character." The promise that this new thing would "spring up" meant it would happen gradually, like the germination and growth of a beautiful wildflower. Its fulfillment would require patience, but its eventuality was sure. That fulfillment would be realized in Jesus.

> **Learning from the past is useful. Dwelling on the past is destructive.**

To be able to look forward with joy, the Israelites needed to let go of the past. The same is true for people today. Learning from the past is useful. Dwelling on the past is destructive. It keeps your focus on things you can no longer change and off what God is doing right before your eyes. Follow Isaiah's advice to the Israelites. Forget what's behind you. Move freely forward toward the good that is sprouting right beneath your feet.

Letting go of past mistakes—yours and those of others—may involve forgiveness, repentance, and reconciliation. Let Isaiah's words encourage you as you work through emotional or relational roadblocks.

Those who love money will never have enough. How absurd to think that wealth brings true happiness! The more you have, the more people come to help you spend it. So what is the advantage of wealth—except perhaps to watch it run through your fingers!

ECCLESIASTES 5:10–11 NLT

Misguided Love

The book of Ecclesiastes includes one of the most important financial truths you'll ever hear. If you love money and the things it can buy, better budgeting, a higher-paying job, or even a winning lottery ticket can't make you happy or alleviate your financial worries. The only deciding factor that you can really depend on is to decide to pursue a fresh, new focus.

Love focuses on what it desires. When you desire God, you spend your time and energy getting to know him better and doing what pleases him. When you desire money, you spend your time and energy fueling an atmosphere of greed, instead of nurturing a sense of contentment. A deep desire for wealth can tempt you to do things you normally wouldn't consider, like cheating, lying, or stealing. You don't need to do anything illegal to fall for temptations like these. All it takes is holding on to the riches God has given you with a tight grip instead of opening

> **Pursuing riches more vigorously than a relationship with your God will lead you to only one place—an impoverished life.**

your arms, and hoarding your blessings instead of sharing them.

The book of Ecclesiastes is all about how meaningless life is apart from God. Pursuing riches more vigorously than a relationship with your God will lead you to only one place— an impoverished life. (Even if your bank account seems to say otherwise!) Instead of focusing on money, focus on God, the source of wealth. Thank him for how he has blessed you, and share what he has so generously given. You will find yourself rich in joy and contentment.

〜

Money promises more than it can ever deliver. God will never do that to you. The treasures he promises his children are both certain and eternal.

God be merciful to us
and bless us, and cause
His face to shine upon us,
that Your way may be
known on earth, Your sal-
vation among all nations.

PSALM 67:1–2 NKJV

Trust in the LORD with all your heart, and lean not on your own understanding.

PROVERBS 3:5 NKJV

Leaning on the Lord

If you are going to lean on something, the first thing you want to do is to make certain it can hold you up. The greater the risk, the more certain you want to be. You may not test the strength of every chair you're considering sitting on, but it's fairly certain that you will test the integrity of a bungee cord before attaching it to your feet and leaping off a bridge. Your trust in the strength and reliability of the bungee cord allows you to lean on its ability to save you. It still may take a lot of courage to go ahead and jump, however.

Believing in God is all about risk and trust. It tells you to turn away from what you're accustomed to relying on—your own strategies for making life work—and instead to trust God implicitly, even when what he's asking you to do may not make sense from a human perspective. Think about what God asked of

Every past experience was once a present choice.

Moses at the Red Sea or of Daniel in the lions' den. Moses and Daniel were able to rely on God instead of on their own understanding because past experience had shown them he was wholly trustworthy.

Every past experience was once a present choice. God challenges you to choose wisely today. You can lean on your own limited understanding and abilities or on a God of unlimited power and love. Only one choice can take you where you really want to go.

Put what you've learned into practice. List why you believe God is trustworthy, focusing on his promises and past faithfulness. Reread the list anytime you need the courage to lean on him instead of on yourself.

The Scripture says, "So a man will leave his father and mother and be united with his wife, and the two will become one body." That secret is very important—I am talking about Christ and the church.

EPHESIANS 5:31–32 NCV

When One Plus One Equals One

When God created woman, he could have fashioned her out of a clump of dirt, just like Adam. He chose instead to create Eve from Adam's side. One became two. Marriage unites the two back into one, while also providing the world with a living, breathing illustration of the relationship between Jesus and the church. No wonder God views marriage as sacred and Paul regarded it as a mysterious secret.

Paul (who was never married) provided principles for a healthy marriage by simply reminding his audience to remember what marriage really is. It is more than a cultural or a legal commitment. It is a fusion that goes deeper than sexual relations. Marriage is a spiritual union of bodies, hearts, and lives. The Scripture Paul

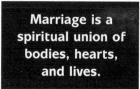

Marriage is a spiritual union of bodies, hearts, and lives.

quoted goes back to the very first marriage between Adam and Eve (Genesis 2:24). It is also quoted by Jesus in the Gospels. When you find a Scripture repeated in several places in the Bible, that should alert you to the fact that something very important is being communicated.

Paul didn't stop with repeating God's original design for marriage. He added that this unique union mimics another unique love relationship, Jesus and the church. If you are looking for advice on how to have a good marriage, you need look no farther than how Jesus and the church were meant to relate, with sacrifice and servanthood.

Marriage is a perfect union between two imperfect people — and like everything else God created, marriage is intrinsically good. Don't study the world to see what marriage should be like. Instead, look at Paul's words.

Where can I go from Your Spirit? Or where can I flee from Your presence? If I ascend into heaven, You are there; if I make my bed in hell, behold, You are there. If I take the wings of the morning, and dwell in the uttermost parts of the sea, even there Your hand shall lead me, and Your right hand shall hold me.

PSALM 139:7–10 NKJV

Ever by Your Side

Like all the other psalms, Psalm 139 voices honest, human emotion in a vibrantly beautiful, truthful, and poetic way. In this one, the psalmist asked rhetorical questions. He was not expressing a desire to get away from God. Quite the contrary. He was emphasizing that if people who wholeheartedly try to escape God's presence have absolutely no possibility of doing it, it would be even more unlikely for a person who is actively drawing close to God to wind up separated from him.

In other words, God is with you everywhere—whether you want him to be or not. This truth is wonderful news for those who long for God. God is always right by your side. His Spirit transcends the limitations of physical space.

This means that you will experience God's presence in a different way than you would the presence of other people. God's Spirit is kind of like oxygen. Once you learn about God's Spirit, you know he is there by his positive effects.

Even though you can't see him, hear him, or feel him, you know that as long as you're breathing, God's Spirit is present. God's Spirit is the oxygen that allows you to be fully alive spiritually. You can see God's Spirit move through answered prayer. You can

> Even though you can't see him, hear him, or feel him, you know that as long as you're breathing, God's Spirit is present.

hear his voice through words of Scripture. You can feel his touch through his gifts of comfort, peace, and joy.

Jesus is often referred to by the name *Immanuel*, meaning "God with us." Psalm 139 shows that God always has and always will be "with us."

One thing I always do. Forgetting the past and straining toward what is ahead, I keep trying to reach the goal and get the prize for which God called me through Christ to the life above.

PHILIPPIANS 3:13–14 NCV

Running to Win

When the apostle Paul said there is "one thing I always do," it is time to sit up and listen. Paul summarized his goal in life and shared a couple of quick tips on how to persevere toward reaching it. That makes his advice not only important, but extremely helpful to those with that same goal in mind.

Paul's images of "straining toward what is ahead" and "trying to reach the goal" paint a picture of a long-distance

runner whose focus on the rewards of the finish line gives him the strength to persevere, one step at a time. The goal Paul pointed to is God's call to run toward a Jesus-centered life, leaving his self-centered life behind in the dust. The prize he longed to reach was not eternal life, because Jesus's death has already achieved that. Instead, Paul pursued a mature Christian life, one that yielded rewards both in heaven and on earth.

> **Keep moving forward—your endurance increases the harder and the farther you run. Keep the finish line in sight.**

Paul's purpose and process for perseverance provide practical applications you can use every day of your life. Put your past mistakes, victories, and self-reliance behind you. Focus your attention and energy on Jesus, not on those running the race alongside you. Keep moving forward—your endurance increases the harder and the farther you run. Keep the finish line in sight. It doesn't mark the end of your life; it marks the beginning of an eternity spent in the winner's circle with Jesus, the One who enables you to be victorious.

Persevering toward maturity in your faith takes both personal effort and the transforming power of God's Spirit. God works through you as you do his work.

I tell you the truth, anything you did for even the least of my people here, you also did for me.

MATTHEW 25:40 NCV

Helping Hands, Healing Hearts

Jesus's disciples questioned him about eternal life and the end of the world. Jesus answered their questions with a series of parables, concluding with one about a herd of sheep and goats. In it, the Son of Man condemned the goats for not meeting his needs: leaving him hungry, thirsty, naked, and lonely when he needed their help most. The sheep were commended for doing what the goats did not—and were surprised by their reward. They didn't remember serving the Son of Man. The words of Matthew 25:40 set the record straight. Any time people reach out to help one of God's children in need, they actually minister to God himself.

This parable is a dialogue between Jesus and the nations of the world, not those who already followed him. That's why the sheep were so amazed. They didn't recognize Jesus or the significance of their actions. They weren't acting out of a desire for reward. They were simply living out God's image in their lives by exhibiting sacrificial love—without even recognizing what they were doing. That truth is why the sheep had a lesson to teach those who already knew God personally.

> **Any time people reach out to help one of God's children in need, they actually minister to God himself.**

This parable assumes that those who follow God will be benevolent and that they will automatically treat others as they would treat Jesus. Experience teaches, however, that isn't always the case. When you notice someone in need, recall Jesus's parable. Be a sheep, not only saved, but motivated by God's love and grace.

The parable of the sheep and goats is a reminder of how eternally significant is every act of love. Allow it to help you to more clearly see Jesus in every person you meet.

Delight yourself also in the Lord, and He shall give you the desires of your heart.

Psalm 37:4 NKJV

Finding Your Heart's Desire

At first glance, the words from Psalm 37 feel a bit like a blank check. They seem to say, "Enjoy God and get everything you want." But instead of a promise of prosperity, the words are a proclamation of a profound truth: the closer you draw to God, the more your desires will reflect his own.

This oft-repeated verse is part of an acrostic psalm, where every other line begins with a successive letter of the Hebrew alphabet. Although each verse in Psalm 37 contains its own unique insight, all the verses work together to convey one important message. Those people who are wise have no need to worry during times of trouble. This psalm gives you four practical ways to defeat worry when evil people seem to be getting ahead: (1) trust in the Lord, (2) commit your way to the Lord, (3) wait on the Lord, and (4) delight in the Lord.

The focus of the psalmist's words is delighting in the Lord. The Hebrew word for *delight* is much more powerful than its English counterpart. Here it means "to find exquisite joy." To delight in God is to find your deepest pleasure, your highest ecstasy, and your richest fulfillment in life through your relationship with him. This is an ongoing process as you

> **The closer you draw to God, the more your desires will reflect his own.**

delight in him afresh each day. As your relationship deepens, what is dear to God's heart becomes dear to your heart. This aligns your prayers with God's will. As your prayers are answered, you discover that your deepest desires are fulfilled.

Any time you desire something that you know would also delight God, spend a moment thanking God for how he's helping you grow to be more like him.

Jesus said, "Go therefore and make disciples of all the nations, baptizing them in the name of the Father and of the Son and of the Holy Spirit, teaching them to observe all things that I have commanded you."

MATTHEW 28:19–20 NKJV

Follow Me

Discipleship is similar to an internship, where hands-on learning comes from closely following the experienced example of another. While on earth, Jesus invited twelve disciples to follow him. For three years they ate with him, drank with him, traveled with him, and prayed with him. They listened and learned through his words and actions. When Jesus rose from the dead, only eleven remained. As Jesus prepared to return to heaven, he challenged those men to put into practice what they'd learned—by making more disciples.

Jesus's mission statement, often referred to as the Great Commission, is directed to everyone who responds to his call to follow him. In the Great Commission, Jesus outlined how his disciples should go and help others grow. First, he explained

In the Great Commission, Jesus outlined how his disciples should go and help others grow.

the scope of their task. In going to "all nations," Jesus assured his disciples that no place on earth was to be exempt from the scope of God's life-changing love.

Second, Jesus instructed his disciples to baptize and to teach. Baptism is a symbol of an inner rebirth that connects new believers with a community of Christians. Teaching budding disciples to focus on Jesus's teaching assured new believers that they would live under the freedom of grace.

Teaching and baptizing a new believer begin the transformation of a new believer into a disciple. However, discipleship is an ongoing process. As you help others mature spiritually, Jesus will bring you to maturity as well.

Helping others find out more about God is Jesus's command for everyone who follows him. Ask God how you can help others see him more clearly.

In [Christ] all the treasures of wisdom and knowledge are safely kept.

COLOSSIANS 2:3 NCV

Buried Treasure

In ancient Colossae, Gnosticism was all the rage. It was a religious cult that promised salvation through secret knowledge that was said to be delivered by angels. Even the group's name was derived from the Greek word for "knowledge," *gnosis*. In his letter to the Colossians, Paul wanted the church to be able to discern what was false from what was true. Instead of seeking secret knowledge, Paul told people to seek Jesus—the source of knowledge itself.

Today people continue to seek the answer to life through intellectual pursuits, philosophical debate, and even angelic revelation. Yet what was true in Paul's day is still true today.

Faith in Jesus is the only road to salvation and to the secrets of life. Faith comes from knowing God through personal experience, not intellectual pursuit. Any knowledge derived from

Knowing God encourages a state of mind that is peaceful and secure.

that perfect source bonds people together in love; they do not pit themselves against one another to show off what they know. Knowing God encourages a state of mind that is peaceful and secure.

Yet this kind of knowledge isn't a treasure trove you acquire the moment you invite God into your life. It is something that's revealed one gem at a time as you dig deeper into the Bible. Focus on Jesus. Get to know him intimately, with your whole being. You'll find knowledge that's practical, eternal, and worth infinitely more than any doctoral degree.

When you act on what you've learned by focusing on Jesus, you demonstrate wisdom. The more you put wisdom to use, the wiser you become.

God so loved the world that He gave His only begotten Son, that whoever believes in Him should not perish but have everlasting life.

JOHN 3:16 NKJV

The Never-Ending Story

John 3:16 has been nicknamed "the Little Gospel." That's because it condenses the message Jesus came to share into a single clear-cut sentence, answering one of the big questions every individual has to face: is there life after death? God's answer to that question is a resounding yes. That truly is "good news," which is what *gospel* literally means.

When you love someone, that love motivates you to give. The same is true with God. God loved the people of the world so deeply that he had to put that love into action. He did that by sending the very best gift he could ever give, a true part of himself—Jesus.

When you love someone, that love motivates you to give. The same is true with God.

Before any gift can be enjoyed, it has to be accepted. People accept God's gift by accepting who Jesus is. That's what belief is all about. But God doesn't stop there. Accepting Jesus comes with an extra bonus gift. That gift is a life that never ends. That gift isn't something people have to wait and open later. Its reality takes hold the moment people accept God's "good news" as a part of their lives. From that moment on, they experience a life that will not end with death but will continue beyond it as they grow ever closer to the One who loves them so deeply—and gave so much because of that love.

Consider a few of the countless ways God has shared his love with you. This generosity will extend from this life into the next. Take a few moments just to say thanks.

Be very careful how you live. Do not live like those who are not wise, but live wisely. Use every chance you have for doing good, because these are evil times.

Ephesians 5:15–16 ncv

Seize the Moment

Life is filled with opportunities—and obstacles that can prevent you from grabbing hold of them. The secret to making the most of your life lies in making the most of your time.

The first three words hold the key: *be very careful*. In the original language, this admonition is much stronger and fuller than what sounds here like a mother's passing comment to her kids as they head outside. The words describe a way of living (or "walking," as the Bible often describes it) that is precise, accurate, and deliberate. It involves both forethought and a heightened sense of awareness. It's similar

to the way you drive a car. You need to
be constantly attentive, responding
appropriately to the ever-changing situations you find yourself in. You
swerve to avoid hazards, brake for
pedestrians, and follow the rules of the

You need to recognize evil, so you can avoid it like a dangerous hazard in the road.

road. Your skill, knowledge, and vigilance help you make
wise decisions at a moment's notice.

To live wisely you need to do the same thing. You need
to face each day spiritually alert. You need to recognize evil,
so you can avoid it like a dangerous hazard in the road. At
the same time, you need to be on the lookout for opportunities to show love to others and to God—and to grab hold of
them. The good news is that God is in the car with you. His
Spirit will help guide your daily journey toward a life full of
well-utilized opportunities.

When you start your car, recall the words from the book of
Ephesians. They can be a reminder to keep your eyes open
for opportunities to make a positive difference throughout
your day.

God is love, and he who abides in love abides in God, and God in him.

1 JOHN 4:16 NKJV

A Love That Never Fails

When it comes to love, the Greek language is incredibly descriptive. It has four different words to distinguish between four kinds of love: the love of friends, familial love, sexual love, and unconditional love. This last kind of love, *agape*, is the one mentioned most frequently in the New Testament. It describes a love bestowed on those who are undeserving, in spite of the possibility of rejection or heartbreak. *Agape* is so unique that, outside the Scriptures, it is found in only one ancient Greek text, where it describes parents' unshakable love for their only child.

God loves you like an only child. His love can't be earned or lost. He loves you simply because you are his. God is more than the source of *agape*. He is *agape*. His very essence, his nature, is love, given without obligation or expectation. He loves unconditionally because that is who he is.

Abide means "to dwell." When you invite God's Spirit to dwell in you, *agape* takes up residence. This gives you the ability to love others the same way God does, without condition. Whether you choose to use that ability is up to you. Unconditional

> **When you invite God's Spirit to dwell in you, *agape* takes up residence.**

love can lead to disappointment and sorrow. It led Jesus to the Cross, but that choice ultimately led to a victory that could not be gained in any other way. Allow *Agape* to help you love unconditionally. Others will catch a glimpse of God through you.

To share *agape*, you have to dwell in God and he in you. That kind of intimate relationship grows through spending time together in prayer and studying Scriptures.

$\mathbf{I}$'m staying alert and in top condition. I'm not going to get caught napping, telling everyone else all about it and then missing out myself.

1 CORINTHIANS 9:27 MSG

The Competitive Edge

The people of Corinth knew all about the self-discipline it takes to become a top athlete. Every two years, the city of Corinth held the Isthmian Games, similar to the Olympics in Athens. Potential athletes trained hard for ten months. If they didn't complete the training or if they broke the rules, they were disqualified from participating in the prestigious competition.

The apostle Paul wanted his readers to understand the same principle was true when it came to going the distance in life. He filled the ninth chapter of his first letter to the Corinthians with boxing and running illustrations that allude to the Isthmian Games. But verse 27 lies at the heart of the passage. It explains why self-discipline is crucial for Christians. When God asks you to do something, you want to be spiritually up to the task. You don't want anything to get in the way of your success. That includes any bad habits, uncontrolled passions, or lazy attitudes.

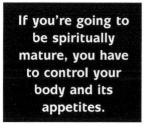

If you're going to be spiritually mature, you have to control your body and its appetites.

Through sheer self-effort, you can discipline your body for athletic competition. Disciplining your body and your soul for spiritual challenges is possible only with God's help. Ask God to show you if there is any area where your lack of self-control could interfere with what he wants you to do. Use Paul's words as an inspiration to gain better discipline in that area.

Like a star athlete who leaves fans disillusioned by acting inappropriately, a Christian who behaves inappropriately can turn others away from God. Let Paul's words remind you that undisciplined words or actions can have serious consequences.

I will praise you every day; I will praise you forever and ever. The LORD is great and worthy of our praise; no one can understand how great he is.

PSALM 145:2–3 NCV

Praise Without End

Creation praises God. Angels praise God. Infants praise God. One day every knee will bow as the whole world praises God. Scripture is filled with examples of praise, especially throughout the book of Psalms. Every one of those verses has a lesson to teach about honoring the Lord of the universe. The specific portion of Psalm 145 is significant because it is like a mini-primer on praise. It tells the who, what, when, where, and why of giving God glory.

The *who* explains God is the One most worthy of your praise. He is so deserving that it is impossible to run out of reasons for praising him. You can praise God for his gifts, but praise is broader than thanksgiving. *What* praise does is honor God for who he is, not just what he does. By honoring God through your prayers and actions you bless him, giving him

Praise cultivates contentment by helping you develop a right view of God and yourself.

pleasure. This alone is a great reason *why* you should praise God (along with the fact he deserves it!). Praise benefits the one giving it, as well as the one receiving it. Praise cultivates contentment by helping you develop a right view of God and yourself.

As for *when* to praise God, Psalm 145 tells you that it is appropriate to praise God every day. The psalm says that you will praise God forever, which means your praises will reach beyond the borders of this earth right into your eternal home in heaven. That's a *where* that you can look forward to.

The Hebrew word for *praising* God means "to celebrate his perfections." Put what you've learned into practice by taking time to do that right now.

Jesus said, "The greatest person in the kingdom of heaven is the one who makes himself humble like this child."

MATTHEW 18:4 NCV

Children at Heart

Jesus's disciples were waiting for a response. They had just asked Jesus an important question, one they sincerely wanted an answer to. It wasn't exactly spiritual in nature. It had to do with position and power. The disciples wanted to know who out of the twelve of them would be the greatest in God's kingdom. Jesus answered them by inviting a small child to sit on his lap. That child became an object lesson in how highly God values humility.

When it comes to power and position, children are at the bottom of the pecking order. They are dependent on others to fill almost every need. They are eager to learn, because they recognize their own ignorance and helplessness. They innocently believe everything they are told, and they share their love freely.

> **Jesus came to earth to make it possible for God's heavenly kingdom to begin here on earth, in the lives of his followers.**

Their goal isn't to be the best. Their goal is simply to be who they are. This is the kind of humble, authentic response that God desires from his own children.

Jesus's poignant words reveal that God's kingdom is vastly different from earthly kingdoms. In it, servants, not celebrities, are honored. Jesus came to earth to make it possible for God's heavenly kingdom to begin on earth. Take a lesson from the child in Jesus's lap. Go to God fully aware of your need and your dependence on him. That's the starting point for nurturing a childlike, humble heart.

—

It is good to want to do great things, but only for the right reason—to bring honor to God, not yourself. Let Jesus's words help you weigh your motives anytime you long to be praised.

You made my whole being; you formed me in my mother's body. I praise you because you made me in an amazing and wonderful way.

PSALM 139:13–14 NCV

Intimately Known

You were a planned pregnancy. You weren't a random egg that just happened to be fertilized by a random spermatozoon. You were—and are—a beloved child, wanted, planned for, and created with a specific purpose and place in this world long before you even entered it. Psalm 139 gives evidence to that fact and is an important touchstone to hold on to any time your self-worth begins to waver.

The Hebrew word *created* means much more than "made." It conveys the joy and pride that come from acquiring an exquisite handmade possession. You were made by an almighty hand with great thought and care. This process is described as "fearful" because of how indescribably awe-inspiring it is. Just thinking about this miracle is enough to bring you to your knees.

That's exactly what it did to David, the writer of this psalm. As David thought about the individual attention to detail God took in creating him, God's goodness and power overwhelmed him. His automatic response was to praise God for what he'd done.

> You were made by an almighty hand with great thought and care.

Consider the miracle of your own creation by considering David's words. Think about the intricacy of the inner workings of your body, your unique physical frame, and the specific personality traits that make you, you. Then do as David did. Thank God for who he created you to be and for the purpose he has for your life.

~~~

Your value isn't determined by your performance, your appearance, or your position in this world. Your value was determined the moment God put his love for you into action by knitting you together.

God said to Moses, "I am who I am."

EXODUS 3:14 NKJV

What's in a Name?

To the people of Israel, a name was more than an iden-
tification for an individual. It was a statement about who
that person was. When Moses (whose name means "taken
from the water") met God for the first time via the burning
bush, Moses wanted to know God's name. Moses wanted to
know who God was. God's reply was "I am." Derived from
the Hebrew verb *to be*, this name let Moses know that the
One he was speaking to was unlike anyone else. God not
only is, but he always was and always will be. God alone

was never created, and he exists totally independent from anyone or anything else. "I am" is the one unchanging, eternal God.

The Jewish people considered God's name so holy that they refused to say it aloud for fear of using it in a way that dishonored him. In the New Testament, however, Jesus not only spoke God's name, but he also used it to refer to himself. The people listening immediately tried to stone Jesus. They knew God's words in

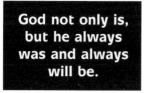

God not only is, but he always was and always will be.

Exodus. They understood that Jesus was calling himself God.

When God told Moses his name, God revealed the essence of who he is—and confirmed in advance that the same essence was in his Son. In the same way that God introduced himself to Moses, this verse introduces you to God. It assures you that the "I am" of the universe is active and involved in life here on earth.

~꧁꧂

Understanding God's eternal nature, and that Jesus is wholly God, gives you the same assurance it did Moses. "I am" is with you, steadfast and unchangeable.

As often as you eat this bread and drink this cup, you proclaim the Lord's death till He comes.

1 CORINTHIANS 11:26 NKJV

Remember Me

Every time you take part in Communion at church, you are preaching a silent sermon. The message you are sharing proclaims the truth that Jesus willingly gave his body and his blood through death on a cross so you could spend eternity with him. It is a message that carries multiple emotions. Sorrow over Jesus's suffering. Joy over his resurrection. Gratitude for the gift of forgiveness and eternal life.

The power of remembrance can become meaningless ritual if you allow your actions to become automatic. That is when you cease to proclaim, or to make public, the message Jesus shared during his Last Supper. It was at that final meal with his disciples that Jesus first used bread and wine as symbols for his own sacrifice. It was there that he explained that his broken body and spilled blood sealed God's New Covenant with his followers. The Old Covenant that temporarily covered a person's sins through animal sacrifice was null and void. The New Covenant of absolute forgiveness was available to all.

> **The power of remembrance can become meaningless ritual if you allow youractions to become automatic.**

Jesus asked his followers to keep on proclaiming this message until his return to earth. While verbal messages communicate to the masses, the silent sermon of verbal messages is actually one you preach to yourself. It is a consistent reminder to stay focused on the basics. You commune with Jesus by looking back at what he did. You look forward to when you'll meet face-to-face. You look within to see what needs to be changed or confessed because of what Jesus has done for you.

Different churches celebrate Communion in different ways. The *how* isn't as important as the *why*, and 1 Corinthians 11:26 clearly points you to the *why*. Keep it in mind every time you celebrate the Lord's Supper.

God said to me, "My grace is sufficient for you, for my power is made perfect in weakness."

2 Corinthians 12:9 NIV

Power Source

Three times the apostle Paul asked God to remove what Paul referred to as a "thorn in the flesh." Some historians speculate that this physical problem was some kind of eye disease. Whatever ailment was troubling Paul, the writer of this letter believed it was interfering with what God wanted him to do. God saw things differently. God will not always answer your prayers in ways you expect. Instead of curing Paul, God answered Paul's prayers by telling him that all Paul needed was God's grace, that God's grace was enough. God may be answering some of your prayers in the very same way.

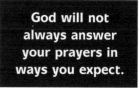

God did not give Paul a reason for the pain he was going through. However, he did give Paul a promise. God promised that the apostle's personal pain would not diminish Paul's impact on the world; rather, his pain would expand it. Having to depend more on God,

> **God will not always answer your prayers in ways you expect.**

and less on his own physical strength and abilities, allowed Paul's life to reveal God's power in a greater way.

Your own personal weakness may be physical, like Paul's. It may come from a lack of confidence in your abilities, a financial setback, or the breakup of a relationship. Whatever struggle you may be facing, God's promise is as true for you as it was for Paul. Your powerlessness to change a situation provides a unique opportunity for God to reveal himself in a more powerful way to you and to those around you.

When you feel that God isn't answering a heartfelt prayer, take a fresh look at the situation. Ask yourself how God's power is evident through your problem. Thank him for what you learn as you persevere.

Jesus answered, "I tell you the truth, unless one is born again, he cannot be in God's kingdom."

JOHN 3:3 NCV

A Brand-New Beginning

The people of Israel were much like people today. They were constantly seeking restoration. They wanted broken bodies made whole. Broken relationships mended. Their broken nation restored to peace and prosperity. Their broken link to eternity reforged. Yet God did not settle for restoration. He sent Jesus to bring regeneration—a totally new life.

This new life is what Jesus was speaking about when he talked to Nicodemus, a Pharisee of rare character who was honestly seeking God's truth. At first Nicodemus misunder-

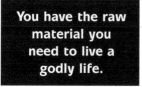

stood the whole concept, arguing that there was no possible way for a baby to reenter his mother's womb and be reborn.

But the birth Jesus was speaking about was a spiritual rebirth, a radical reawakening to who you were created to be. The spiritual rebirth was a brand-new way of relating to life that is possible only through the gift of a totally new nature.

> **You have the raw material you need to live a godly life.**

The "old" nature was focused on self. The "new" nature is focused on God. Like a newborn who is predisposed toward certain traits because of his DNA but nonetheless has to positively participate in the maturity process to reach his potential, you have the raw material you need to live a godly life. To mature in that life, you must choose to nurture your new nature. Nourish yourself with the Bible. Exercise your spiritual muscles by acting on what God asks you to do. Rest in God's promise that the past is gone and that you have been born again.

Use Jesus's words as a touchstone anytime you get discouraged about how long it takes to become spiritually mature. You have the right DNA. Adulthood is inevitable. It just takes time to get there.

Jesus said to those Jews who believed Him, "If you abide in My word, you are My disciples indeed. And you shall know the truth, and the truth shall make you free."

JOHN 8:31–32 NKJV

Free at Last

In today's postmodern society, talking about truth can be tricky. If you want to discuss *a* truth, feel free. However, talking about *the* truth is a whole other matter. Talking about the truth would imply that what you're sharing is an absolute truth, something that is true for everyone—whether everyone personally believes it to be true or not.

That's the kind of truth Jesus was talking about to his Jewish audience in the temple treasury as recorded in the Gospel of John. The term Jesus used for *truth* was the same one used to describe a legal standard, a fact that would stand up in court. This fact was broader than just the truth about who Jesus was. The Jews who were listening already believed. The truth Jesus spoke of is the kind revealed over the course of a lifetime, as those who believe in him choose to obey his words.

In ancient Greek, *know* means more than "to make a mental note of." It means that you have tested your belief experientially. By putting Jesus's teaching into practice, you can come to know the truth about God, life, and yourself. This knowledge frees you from chains you may not even be aware are holding you back, such chains as pride, selfishness, and the

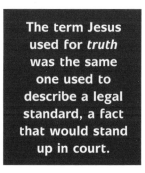

The term Jesus used for *truth* was the same one used to describe a legal standard, a fact that would stand up in court.

temptation to do what is contrary to Jesus's words. Let God's truth lead you to true freedom today.

~

God's promise of freedom is linked to putting his words to the test. Get to know his words better by reading, meditating on, and praying about at least one verse of Scripture each day.

Submit to one another out of reverence for Christ.

Ephesians 5:21 NLT

Willing Surrender

For many people, the idea of submitting themselves to someone else carries negative connotations. Submitting implies inferiority, subservience, or blind obedience. Nothing could be farther from God's truth. Submission as described in the Bible is a mutual commitment between two equals whose goal is to foster unity and cooperation. The ancient Greek word used in the Bible to describe submission is a military command telling troops to get in order according to their rank. By following this structure of authority, soldiers can work together more efficiently to accomplish their own individual duties. A company with too many generals and not enough privates has little chance of winning a war.

In the Bible, several verses ask wives to submit to their husbands, servants to submit to their masters, and citizens to submit to the government. Ephesians 5:21 lays the groundwork for them all. It makes absolutely clear that submission is

In daily life, submitting to one another looks a lot like respect, humility, and love.

expected of every follower of Jesus, not just a few specific groups of people. One way that Jesus showed his love was by willingly setting his rights aside to better serve others. Every time you follow his example, you honor him.

In daily life, submitting to one another looks a lot like respect, humility, and love. It means that demanding your own way, flaunting your authority, or nurturing a superiority complex are things of the past. It means that your life is beginning to look more like Jesus's.

—

Before mutual submission is evident in your actions, it needs to take root in your attitude. That process begins the moment you submit your own personal agenda for life to God's.

We . . . have joy with our troubles, because we know that these troubles produce patience. And patience produces character, and character produces hope.

ROMANS 5:3–4 NCV

Character Under Pressure

Genuine diamonds are known for both their beauty and their strength. Though they begin as common carbon, constant pressure over an extended period of time creates something of rare value. The same is true for strength of character, which is just as rare and even more valuable. True character exhibits integrity through consistent moral excellence. Through the apostle Paul's words, God shares the secret of how this priceless character trait is developed. It takes place through an unexpected process—experiencing joy when you're suffering under pressure.

In several versions of the Bible, the word for *suffering* is translated "tribulation." This comes from the Latin word *tribulum*, which was taken from the name of a piece of farm equipment used during New Testament times. A tribulum was a heavy piece of timber with spikes in it that was drawn over newly picked grain. It separated the valuable grain from the worthless chaff. Tribulation, or suffering, does the

True character exhibits integrity through consistent moral excellence.

same thing to your character. It sifts it, helping you sort out what's truly important in life from what's of little value.

As your character grows stronger, so does your hope. Experiencing firsthand how God can use difficult circumstances in a positive way solidifies your hope for the future as it strengthens your trust in him. This character-building process hones the resulting hope by persevering through difficulties. This is what allows you to find genuine joy, even in the middle of suffering.

―◦◦◦

A diamond has no choice in how it responds to pressure. You do. Choosing to focus on the hope that produces joy during hard times develops a character that's more like Jesus's own.

Put on the whole armor of God, that you may be able to stand against the wiles of the devil. For we do not wrestle against flesh and blood, but against principalities, against powers, against the rulers of the darkness of this age.

EPHESIANS 6:11–12 NKJV

Wrestling with Evil

When wrestlers compete, they rely on both strength and strategy to overcome their opponent. Even before the match begins, a wrestler takes a moment to size up his opponent, looking for his opponent's potential vulnerabilities, while remaining fully aware of his own. The passage in Ephesians uses the image of a wrestling match to convey the ongoing struggle and preparation that standing strong against evil entails—and it reminds you to be sure that you are fighting the right opponent.

People may do evil things, but your battle is not with individuals. Your battle is with evil itself. The Ephesians were well-acquainted with principalities, powers, and rulers of darkness— different kinds of evil spirits. The society was heavily involved in sorcery and magic. Even those who chose not

> People may do evil things, but your battle is not with individuals. Your battle is with evil itself.

to follow God were aware there was some kind of spiritual battle going on behind the scenes of their everyday lives. Ephesians 6 provides readers with God's guidelines on how to effectively fight that battle.

Mixing metaphors between wrestling and fighting a battle, Ephesians 6 instructs you to cover yourself with God-given armor. This protective gear is described in more detail in subsequent verses, but it includes things such as truth, righteousness, God's Spirit, God's Word, and prayer. As you choose to don God's armor each day and remind yourself who your opponent really is, you'll find yourself well-prepared to hold your ground against evil.

Being prepared to encounter evil and focusing on it are two different things. Stay focused on God. His Spirit will make you aware of any battles you need to face.

Faith means being sure of the things we hope for and knowing that something is real even if we do not see it. Faith is the reason we remember great people who lived in the past.

HEBREWS 11:1–2 NCV

The Power of Faith

Faith and belief are two different things. Lots of people believe in God, but that belief makes no difference in their lives. Faith, however, acts on what it believes. Faith may look like a "leap" to those who don't want to risk putting their trust in something unseen. But through faith, what is unseen is far from unknown. As you actively respond to the Bible and God's Spirit, your faith continues to grow stronger. Your personal experience confirms that God is everything he says he is.

Hebrews 11:1–2 is the introduction to a section of Scripture known as the Hall of Faith. The list of ancients that follows includes people like Moses, Noah, and Abraham, people who are remembered for putting their beliefs to the test. The Jewish Christians this letter was written for complained that following God was too difficult for ordinary people. The truth found in these verses refutes that claim.

Faith in God is what sets ordinary people apart—like Moses, Noah, and Abraham—so they can do extraordinary things. Through simple trust and active obedience, faith makes unseen spiritual realities more visible. Faith is what makes them *certain*, which in Greek is a legal term similar to a title deed that guarantees a possession will be yours in the future. You have God's guarantee that what he has promised

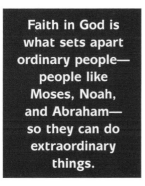

Faith in God is what sets apart ordinary people— people like Moses, Noah, and Abraham— so they can do extraordinary things.

will be yours. The faithfulness of that guarantee is what makes the foundation of your faith sturdy enough to step forward in confidence.

Faith follows four steps: (1) God speaks, (2) you hear, (3) you trust, (4) you act. As you repeat these steps day by day, you'll be writing your own unique chapter in the Hall of Faith.

God said to me, "My grace is sufficient for you, for my power is made perfect in weakness."

2 CORINTHIANS 12:9 NIV

We all, with unveiled face, beholding as in a mirror the glory of the Lord, are being transformed into the same image from glory to glory.

2 Corinthians 3:18 nkjv

Extreme Makeover

In the Old Testament, when God gave Moses the Ten Commandments, Moses was allowed to catch a glimpse of the unique splendor of God's actual presence. This experience was so profound that Moses's face literally glowed as a result. The Israelites who followed Moses were frightened by the change in his appearance and by a God who could transform someone in that way. But Moses's transformation was temporary. At first Moses veiled his face so that the people would no longer be afraid. Later he wore the veil to conceal the fact that his personal evidence of God's glory was fading away.

God's glory refers both to God's unfathomable beauty and to his incomparable expression of power. As you look into God's mirror, which is a biblical synonym that stands for the Bible, you glimpse what Moses did. You see God. Unlike Moses, the reflection of God's glory in you will never fade. In fact, it will continue to shine brighter as time

God's glory refers both to God's unfathomable beauty and to his incomparable expression of power.

goes by. You are not being transformed into God; you are being transformed into a sharper reflection of his image.

This means you don't need to hide behind a veil when you're with others. Be honest and authentic, freely sharing how God is working in your life. In this way, you become a spiritual mirror for those around you as you grow to look more and more like your heavenly Father.

As God becomes more visible in you, you'll find that people are naturally attracted to you—not simply because of the wonderful way God created you, but because of how glorious God is.

Christ accepted you, so you should accept each other, which will bring glory to God.

ROMANS 15:7 NCV

Without Reservation

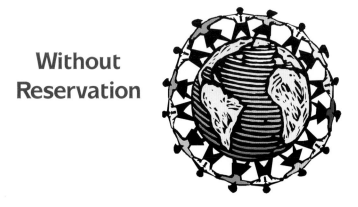

The church in Rome was divided. People were accepting certain religious customs and truths about God but rejecting others. They were doing the same to the people who followed them. Their condescending attitudes were out of line with God's purpose and perspective. That truth is as valid today as it was almost two thousand years ago.

Jesus accepted everyone without reservation. He knew everyone inside and out—he knew the good, the bad, and everything in between. He accepted you long before you

noticed him, even if you rejected him, and solely because he loves you unconditionally.

As you grow more intimate with the One who has fully accepted you, it becomes easier to accept those around you, even those whose actions, attitudes, and beliefs do not line up with your own. You may not condone what they do or agree with what they believe, but you can still receive them with open arms, which is what the Greek word for *accept* really means. Being

> **Being honest, authentic, and accepting in your love, even of people who misunderstand or reject you, helps them see what God's love is like.**

honest, authentic, and accepting in your love, even of people who misunderstand or reject you, helps them see what God's love is like. It gives them a real-life picture of how Jesus related to others—and ultimately relates to them. When you accept others, it pleases God, as well as reveals him.

Pray for anyone you have difficulty accepting. Ask God to reveal any fear, anger, or jealousy on your part. Then ask God to help you understand how he feels about the one you're praying for.

Jesus wept.

JOHN 11:35 NKJV

Telltale Tears

Out of all the creatures in God's creation, only people cry. Tears often say what words cannot. When Jesus cried outside the tomb of his friend Lazarus, Jesus's humanity cried out as loudly as his divinity would moments later when Jesus raised his friend from the dead.

Jesus's tears were different from those of many of the mourners surrounding him. Those people were wailing in accordance with Jewish custom. This tradition allowed the community to fulfill a duty to publicly and loudly lament personal tragedy more so than it allowed those who were grieving a personal release of emotion. The Greek word used here for *wept* is found nowhere else in Scripture. It means "to cry silently." Jesus didn't cry for the benefit of others. He didn't cry to make a point or to teach a lesson. He cried because his heart was broken.

God's heart breaks because he has compassion for those he has created. That means he does not take your pain, sorrow, grief, disappointment, or even physical death lightly. God knows he can bring good out of tragedy and enjoy eternal life with you after your days on earth are through, just as Jesus knew he could raise Lazarus from the dead. That doesn't stop God

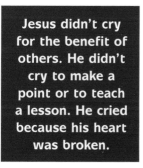

Jesus didn't cry for the benefit of others. He didn't cry to make a point or to teach a lesson. He cried because his heart was broken.

from entering into your present sorrow with you, from reaching out in compassion to bring comfort when you need it most. When you cry, cry out to him.

Jesus was not ashamed to express his emotions and let others see him cry. Follow his example of honest emotional vulnerability, while inviting him to help dry your tears from the inside out.

I have learned to be satisfied with the things I have and with everything that happens. I know how to live when I am poor, and I know how to live when I have plenty. I have learned the secret of being happy at any time in everything that happens . . . I can do all things through Christ, because he gives me strength.

PHILIPPIANS 4:11–13 NCV

Satisfaction Guaranteed

The apostle Paul was born into wealth and privilege. As an adult, he was a Jewish religious leader who wielded power that demanded respect. When Paul chose to follow Jesus, he experienced a new set of circumstances, hunger, poverty, persecution, and imprisonment. When Paul wrote to the church at Philippi about learning how to find contentment, his firsthand experience made him reliable.

One reason Paul shared this life lesson was to dispute Stoic philosophy, which was very popular at the time. When Paul spoke about learning the secret, he was using the same term the Stoics used when initiating members into their cult.

Their secret to successful living was based on total self-sufficiency and a dispassionate acceptance of what life brought their way. Their "whatever" philosophy offered self-centered resignation. Paul's alternative was God-centered contentment.

Experiencing genuine joy and contentment when life is difficult is possible only when you lean on God's strength instead of your own. As you get closer to God, you see things more from his point of view. Your gratitude grows as you become more aware of  the blessings he brings your way every day. And when things are going well, you don't worry about what would happen if you lost it all. You know that no matter what happens, you've found the secret to living a contented life.

Being afraid of what misfortune the future may hold can keep you stuck in the darkness of depression or anxiety.

Deepen your own sense of contentment by spending a few moments right now thanking God for the material, emotional, physical, and spiritual blessings he has brought your way over the last week.

Samuel answered, "What pleases the LORD more: burnt offerings and sacrifices or obedience to his voice? It is better to obey than to sacrifice. It is better to listen to God than to offer the fat of sheep."

1 SAMUEL 15:22 NCV

The Gift of Obedience

Samuel was a prophet in Old Testament times who boldly challenged Israel's king with God's truth as voiced in this verse. King Saul and Israel's armies had just defeated the Amalekites, old enemies who continually threatened the Israelites' way of life. God had told Saul to conquer the Amalekites and to totally destroy their flocks and possessions. Saul and his men obeyed God to a point. They destroyed sick animals and worthless goods, but they kept what was valuable for themselves. When Samuel confronted Saul's disobedience, the king defended his actions, saying he didn't intend to keep the animals but was going to sacrifice them to God.

Samuel's reply to Saul's unconvincing excuse clearly illustrates what matters most to God. When you choose to disobey God, your worship cannot be wholehearted or sincere. When you actively listen to God by doing what he asks, you give

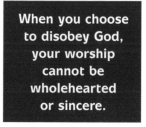

When you choose to disobey God, your worship cannot be wholehearted or sincere.

God a gift he treasures even more than your sacrifice and praise—your heart.

Saul responded to Samuel's words by admitting to God how wrong he had been. God forgave him, but he allowed Saul to suffer the consequences of his disobedience. Saul's greed and deceit cost him the throne. God can use you only to the degree that you obey him. The more deeply you love him, the more you'll want to do what he asks and the more you'll end up pleasing him.

Think of a time in your life when someone was a "Samuel" to you, helping you turn from disobedience to obedience. Take a moment to thank God for that person.

Though I walk through the valley of the shadow of death, I will fear no evil; for You are with me; Your rod and Your staff, they comfort me.

PSALM 23:4 NKJV

In the Shepherd's Care

The Twenty-third Psalm is familiar to many people because they've heard its comforting words recited at the funeral of a loved one. Though the rest of the psalm carries peaceful images of the Lord as a shepherd, green pastures, quiet streams, and an overflowing banquet table, verse 4 is the heart of the psalm and is one of the Bible's most powerful truths to combat fear.

In the original Hebrew language, *the valley of the shadow of death* literally translates into "the valley of deep darkness." Death is only one kind of "deep darkness." There are many other dark times people fear to pass through, such valleys as illness, unemployment, or rejection. The landscape of some valleys is not carved out of actual circumstances but out of fear itself. Being afraid of what misfortune the future may hold can keep you stuck in the darkness of depression or anxiety. It prevents you from walking through the valley to the other side.

> Being afraid of what misfortune the future may hold can keep you stuck in the darkness of depression or anxiety.

The secret to alleviating fear is remembering that you never have to face your fears alone. Your Good Shepherd, the all-powerful God, is right there with you, rod and staff in hand. A shepherd uses a rod to protect his flock from predators. He uses a staff to guide stray sheep back onto the proper path. God figuratively uses these shepherding tools as he keeps you safe and headed in the right direction. By staying close to him, you'll discover comfort and courage close at hand when you find the struggles of life, and death, directly in your path.

—⟡—

At the first hint of fear, picture God as your loving Shepherd, fighting off whatever you fear with his rod and nudging you closer to him with his staff.

We've been given a glimpse of the real thing, our true home, our resurrection bodies! The Spirit of God whets our appetite by giving us a taste of what's ahead. He puts a little of heaven in our hearts so that we'll never settle for less.

2 CORINTHIANS 5:4–5 MSG

A Taste of Home

Think of the best meal you've ever eaten. Recall its appearance, its flavor, its aroma. Chances are you can't remember exactly how it tasted. All you know is that you loved it. Although you can't totally recapture the experience of this gastronomic delight, simply thinking about it certainly gets those salivary glands going. Just the thought can make you long for more.

That is what God's Spirit makes you feel about heaven. You've been given a taste of paradise through brief descriptions in the Bible. Furthermore, God's Spirit has awakened a hunger in your heart that your mind can't fully comprehend. Your heart longs for the home you were created to inhabit, a place where death, pain, and sorrow have no hold, where your body is healthy and whole, where peace and

By keeping heaven in your heart and on your mind, you'll gain strength to handle life here and now, as you rest in the fact that God's best is yet to come.

praise replace struggle and strife, where you meet God face-to-face and never have to say good-bye.

Heaven is as real as those God-given longings. But God didn't give you a taste of what's ahead to leave you discontented with where you are now. He uses those longings as a homing device to keep you headed in the right direction. By keeping heaven in your heart and on your mind, you'll gain strength to handle life here and now, as you rest in the fact that God's best is yet to come.

Think about what difference it makes to your life here on earth to know that heaven is real. Thank God for each reason that comes to mind.

We are His workmanship, created in Christ Jesus for good works, which God prepared beforehand that we should walk in them.

EPHESIANS 2:10 NKJV

Master Plan

You are God's poem. The Greek word for *workmanship* is *poïēma*, from which the English word *poem* is derived. This term does not refer to your original creation in the womb; rather, it refers to a spiritual birth, a rewriting of your life by the hand of God's Spirit as you allow him to guide you each day. Just as every literal poem differs in meter, tone, and message, you, too, have a unique purpose and place in this world.

Before a poet puts pen to paper, he decides what the overall purpose of his poem will be. Then he considers which format and style would work best to convey his message. In the same way, God considers how your unique life and gifts can best make a positive impact on the world. Then God prepares opportunities for you, practical ways you can put his love into action.

God prepares opportunities for you, practical ways you can put his love into action.

However, unlike a literary masterpiece, a living-breathing poem can choose to edit itself. You have the freedom to use these God-given opportunities or to ignore them. What you do, or choose not to do, does not affect your eternal destiny. The more consistently you choose to obey the way God leads you, the deeper your own faith and sense of purpose in this life will be — and the more beautiful and effectual a poem you will become.

Your own effort and creativity play a part in determining the exact nature of the good things you'll do. God's Spirit working through you as you act is what makes your good works great.

Come near to God, and God will come near to you. You sinners, clean sin out of your lives. You who are trying to follow God and the world at the same time, make your thinking pure.

JAMES 4:8 NCV

Looking for Love in All the Right Places

Drawing closer to someone you can't see, touch, or hear in a physical sense is naturally going to be a bit different from any other relationship you've ever experienced. That's why God has given you guidelines on how you can know him better. What makes these simple instructions even more important is the fact they come with a promise: if you embrace God more closely, he'll do the same with you.

The two rules the apostle James offered are applicable whether you've allowed God's Spirit to work in your life for years or have only just begun to have an interest in knowing God more intimately. At their core, these rules are not all that different from how you build a relationship with anyone you love. First, you choose to do the right thing. When you love others, you honor them by

Draw closer to God today by allowing your actions and your attitudes to reflect your heartfelt love.

treating them the way they deserve. You make sure your actions reflect the sincerity of your love.

Second, you also need to maintain a right attitude along with right actions. When you choose to follow God, you make a U-turn from following the way much of the rest of the world lives. Returning to a mind-set of greed, lust, and pride, instead of one based on generosity, love, and humility, is like focusing on an old, abusive relationship when you are involved in a new, healthy one. It is a barrier toward moving forward. Draw closer to God today by allowing your actions and your attitudes to reflect your heartfelt love.

Consider what you have done to draw closer to God over the past year. Then think about what tangible way you feel God has drawn closer to you.

Jesus said, "I am the way, the truth, and the life. No one comes to the Father except through Me."

JOHN 14:6 NKJV

One Way

It was the night of the Last Supper. The apostle Judas had just left to betray Jesus to the religious authorities. Jesus had just predicted his own death and Peter's upcoming denial of knowing him. Undoubtedly, the remaining apostles were overwhelmed with what they heard, even though they didn't understand it fully. Jesus wanted to calm their fears, so he spoke to them about heaven, assuring his friends that he was preparing a special place for each of them. But Thomas was still apprehensive. He asked Jesus

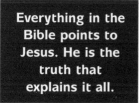
how they would know how to get to where Jesus was. Those words were Jesus's powerful reply.

The only way to heaven, eternal life, and God himself, is through Jesus. After Jesus' death, the message his followers shared with others was often referred to as "the Way." The focus of this message was that Jesus fulfilled what the Scriptures

> **Everything in the Bible points to Jesus. He is the truth that explains it all.**

promised. His death opened the way for people's rebellion against God to be forgiven so they could spend eternity together with him.

Jesus is the living truth of this message. He is the way God has communicated most clearly with the world. No other person, religious belief, tradition, or philosophy contains the whole story, the complete truth about God and the meaning of life. Everything in the Bible points to Jesus. He is the truth that explains it all. Only by responding to that truth can an authentic, purpose-filled life be yours—in this world and the next.

Some people believe Jesus was just a good man. If you speak to anyone who believes this, ask what he or she feels about Jesus in light of what John 14:6 says.

The person who plants a little will have a small harvest, but the person who plants a lot will have a big harvest . . . You should not be sad when you give, and you should not give because you feel forced to give . . . God can give you more blessings than you need. Then you will always have plenty of everything— enough to give to every good work.

2 CORINTHIANS 9:6–8 NCV

Giving That Grows

There are three types of givers in this world: sad, mad, and glad. God delights in those who give *happily*, which literally translates "hilariously." Hilarious giving is not determined by the size of a gift, but by the motive of the giver. A farmer plants his field because he is motivated by the harvest it will yield. He knows that the more seeds he plants, the better chance there will be of an abundant harvest. In

the same way, those who give generously plant their financial seeds with a purpose. They know God will use their gifts to bring about spiritual growth in themselves and others, so they give happily and regularly.

It's true that God promises to give back to those who give. That doesn't mean that everyone who gives financially will receive more material

Blessings come in many forms, from opportunities and abilities to contentment and delight.

wealth in return, however. Blessings come in many forms, from opportunities and abilities to contentment and delight. God expects that his generosity to you will inspire you to be generous to others.

Remember who handed you the seed in the first place. Everything you own is God's gift to you. As you hold on loosely, and gratefully, to what he's given, he will guide you toward when, where, and how you can best share what you have with others. As you follow his lead, you will be worshiping God through your actions, giving a priceless gift back to him.

Ask God to help you clearly see if you are a sad, mad, or glad giver. Then ask him to guide you in how to give more hilariously.

Let brotherly love continue. Do not forget to entertain strangers, for by so doing some have unwittingly entertained angels.

HEBREWS 13:1–2 NKJV

Open-Door Policy

In biblical times, practicing hospitality meant more than inviting your best friends over for dinner. Quite frequently it meant opening your door to a stranger. Long before mass transit, travelers often had to spend the night in an unfamiliar town as they journeyed from one place to another. In the early days of the church, many people were persecuted for their newfound faith in Jesus. Many were rejected by their families and in need of a place to stay. A practical way Christians loved one another was by extending their hospitality, often to those they'd never met. The Greek word for *hospitality* actually means "the love of strangers."

Today, though circumstances have changed, strangers are still in need of love. They may not show up unannounced at your door, but they are nearby if you simply open your eyes and your heart. A new neighbor, a visitor to your church, or even a child who needs foster care may be just the person God is asking you to make feel right at home.

The Bible says that even angels are occasional houseguests. This happened several times in the Old Testament to people like Abraham, Lot, and Gideon—and it could happen to you. However, angels are simply God's messengers. God uses people more frequently than angels when he wants to communicate

God may have a special message he wants you to hear, and the guest you invite to dinner may be just the one to deliver it.

with someone. God may have a special message he wants you to hear, and the guest you invite to dinner may be just the one to deliver it.

Pray God would help you become more aware of the people around you who could use your help, particularly those whom you don't know well. Ask one of them to dinner sometime this month.

Christ accepted you, so you should accept each other, which will bring glory to God.

ROMANS 15:7 NCV

Jesus read, "The Spirit of the LORD is upon Me, because He has anointed Me to preach the gospel to the poor; He has sent Me to heal the brokenhearted, to proclaim liberty to the captives and recovery of sight to the blind, to set at liberty those who are oppressed; to proclaim the acceptable year of the LORD."

LUKE 4:18–19 NKJV

Everlasting Liberty

Jesus was back in his hometown of Nazareth, after recently being baptized by John the Baptist. It was Saturday, the Sabbath, so Jesus went to the synagogue, as was the Jewish custom. There men read from the Scriptures and commented on what they'd read. Jesus was handed the scroll of the Old Testament prophet Isaiah, and he chose to read the words from Isaiah 61:1 to the crowd. Afterward he said, "Today this Scripture has been fulfilled in your hearing." This was the beginning of Jesus's public outreach to the people of Israel and to the world.

About seven hundred years before Jesus was born, the prophet Isaiah recorded the future Messiah's purpose statement. *Messiah* means "Anointed One," or someone God has set apart for a very special purpose. Jesus's special purpose was to extend God's freedom to those who were in captivity. In Isaiah's time, the prophet's words

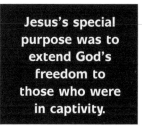

Jesus's special purpose was to extend God's freedom to those who were in captivity.

comforted those who had experienced literal captivity. They had been exiled from their home and forced to live under the harsh rule of the Babylonians.

In Jesus's time, Jesus did set some people free from the bondage of physical and mental ailments. However, the liberty Jesus was destined to deliver goes much deeper than that. He fulfilled Isaiah's words by providing freedom from spiritual blindness and the power of sin and death. The freedom Jesus offers is permanent. Once he breaks the invisible chains that are holding you back, you have the freedom to become who God created you to be.

Think back over your life, calling to mind what spiritual, physical, or emotional chains God has freed you from. Thank him for the liberty he's given you in each of those areas.

No one ever hates his own body, but feeds and takes care of it. And that is what Christ does for the church, because we are parts of his body.

EPHESIANS 5:29–30 NCV

Body Building

The church is not a building with steeples and stained glass. The church is a group of people who are so closely joined to Jesus and to one another that they work together as if they are one single body. The people may meet in a building, complete with steeples, every Sunday, or they may meet in private homes, public schools, or even outdoors. It doesn't matter where they meet. What matters is what happens when they do.

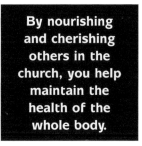

The care of both the local church and the international church as a whole is of primary concern to Jesus. If you are a part of that church body, you will feel about it as Jesus does. You'll want to give the same attention to taking care of those you're intimately connected with as you do to taking care of yourself.

The Greek word for *feed* means more than just supplying nutrition. It means nourishing every internal need. This includes spiritual and emotional needs, as well as the food you digest internally. *Take care of* means "to cherish." It is a very rare ancient Greek word that is found only

> **By nourishing and cherishing others in the church, you help maintain the health of the whole body.**

once outside Scripture on a marriage contract written on papyrus. In its most literal sense, *cherish* means "to take care of every external need someone else has." By nourishing and cherishing others in the church, you help maintain the health of the whole body.

In the Old Testament, the people of Israel were referred to by a Hebrew word that translates as the "congregation." It means the complete assembly of God's people. Your local congregation is not complete without you.

Love must be sincere. Hate what is evil; cling to what is good. Be devoted to one another in brotherly love. Honor one another above yourselves.

ROMANS 12:9–10 NIV

The Real Thing

In the Middle East during biblical times, clay pots were a valuable resource. They were also fragile. It wasn't uncommon for pots to receive a crack or two on the way to the marketplace, which meant they were no longer watertight. Sometimes merchants would fill in the cracks with wax and try to pass the pots off as unblemished. Because of that unscrupulous practice, pots that were whole and complete were referred to as *sincere*, meaning "without wax."

Hypocrites are cracked pots, riddled with wax. They try to pass themselves off as something they're not. Being authentic means being sincere in the way you relate to others. This means letting people see you for who you really are. It also means treating others in a way that reflects who they really are—unique individuals dearly loved by God.

Love has to be sincere. If it isn't, it isn't love at all. The verses that follow this passage paint a picture of what a sincere person looks like: patient, prayerful, hospitable, generous, empathic, a true servant. But the key to all these characteristics

Being authentic means being sincere in the way you relate to others.

lies in a person's sincerity. Being an authentically sincere person doesn't mean you're perfect. It simply means that people who are real before God allow more of God's character to shine through them. God's Spirit gives you the combination of courage and humility it takes to be open and honest with others and to keep your character wax-free.

Jesus was totally authentic in the way he related to people. His sincerity helped make him an approachable and reliable teacher and friend. Consider how authenticity affects your own relationships.

Jesus went a little farther and fell on His face, and prayed, saying, "O My Father, if it is possible, let this cup pass from Me; nevertheless, not as I will, but as You will."

MATTHEW 26:39 NKJV

Choosing God's Way

Jesus knew what his heavenly Father wanted him to do. The primary purpose of his time on earth was to sacrifice his life to save others. The time was drawing near when that purpose would be fulfilled. Jesus did what he always did when faced with a stressful situation. He prayed.

Jesus's prayer in the Garden of Gethsemane reveals the internal struggle he was facing. Throughout the Bible, the phrase *God's cup* figuratively holds either blessing or punishment. The cup before Jesus held the punishment the entire world deserved—separation from God. When Jesus asked

God to remove "this cup," he was not wrestling with what God wanted him to accomplish. If Jesus wanted to avoid arrest, all he had to do was go into hiding. During the Passover season, Jerusalem was filled with pilgrims. Jesus could have easily avoided his familiar routines and blended in with the crowd. Instead, he went to the Garden of Gethsemane to pray, as he was known to do.

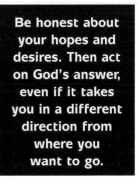

Be honest about your hopes and desires. Then act on God's answer, even if it takes you in a different direction from where you want to go.

In that garden, Jesus asked God to revise his plans. Jesus felt free to ask for what he wanted, but willingly accepted God's answer, whatever it would be. When you want to know what God wants you to do, follow Jesus's example. Be honest about your hopes and desires. Then act on God's answer, even if it takes you in a different direction from where you want to go. God sees the big picture. You can trust him to lead you where you need to go.

God may ask you to do difficult things. Feel free to ask him to provide another way. Just remember that his answer may be to provide the strength you need to move ahead as planned.

Since God has shown us great mercy, I beg you to offer your lives as a living sacrifice to him. Your offering must be only for God and pleasing to him, which is the spiritual way for you to worship.

ROMANS 12:1 NCV

A Thank-You Note to God

When it comes to worship, who you are matters more than what you do. If you are someone who deeply loves God and wants to live a life that gives him joy, everything you do can be a form of worship. From singing songs of praise to washing dishes or helping out a friend, every moment of your life becomes a thank-you gift to God.

Giving these simple gifts or offerings comes naturally when you give God one big gift each day—the gift of your life. In the Old Testament, people gave God their first fruits.

This was a thank-you gift given to God in return for all he'd given them. They'd give the first and best portion of produce they'd harvested, riches they'd received, or the best animals from their flocks. After Jesus sacrificed his life for others, God asked people to follow his Son's example by presenting him with the gift of themselves. You don't have to die to give this gift. All you have to do is ask God to help you devote your body, mind, and heart to becoming who he wants you to be. That's how you turn an ordinary life into a dynamic living sacrifice.

> From singing songs of praise to washing dishes or helping out a friend, every moment of your life becomes a thank-you gift to God.

To worship God simply means to declare him worthy of the honor you are giving him. When you give God your life, you are honoring him with the very best of what he has given you, your ultimate first fruits.

Worship is not just a gift to God, but it is also a gift to yourself. It helps you see things more clearly from his point of view while enjoying a deeper sense of his presence in your life.

Y̲ou were sealed with the Holy Spirit of promise, who is the guarantee of our inheritance.

EPHESIANS 1:13–14 NKJV

Signed, Sealed, and Delivered

God's Spirit is his active presence working in you, through you, and around you in this world. He is also an irrevocable seal and guarantee of your spiritual heritage and eternal destiny. The seal of God's Spirit in your life is like a brand, identifying you as a genuine child of God. In the same way that an official seal can signify that an important transition is complete, God's Spirit is proof that Jesus has paid the full price to purchase your life.

God's Spirit is more than a just a sign to you and the world that God will keep his promises to you. God's Spirit is your personal guarantee of wonderful things ahead. The Greek word that is translated "guarantee" is still used today in Greece to refer to an engagement ring. When you get engaged, you make a mutual promise to commit to spend the future together with someone you love. Though an engaged couple are already in love, the intimacy of their current relationship cannot come close to what it will be after they are united in marriage.

> **God's Spirit is your personal guarantee of wonderful things ahead.**

The same is true with your relationship with God. You may love him now and draw close to him in prayer through the presence of his Spirit. However, your future union in heaven will be much more intimate than anything you can experience here on earth. Right now, think of God's Spirit as your engagement ring, a powerful reminder of God's commitment to share forever with you.

Consider what kind of inheritance awaits you in heaven: life and love that never end, a new body, a new heaven and earth. Thank God for what the presence of his Spirit means in your life.

He who follows righteousness and mercy finds life, righteousness and honor.

PROVERBS 21:21 NKJV

Walking in God's Footsteps

Righteousness is more than just doing the right thing. It is being the right person, which begins by being in a right relationship with God. To get a clear picture of what righteousness looks like—to be able to follow after it—involves taking a close look at God's character as revealed throughout Scripture. What you'll find is pure integrity.

When a building has integrity, it means that its foundation and construction are sound. Its walls and doorframes are straight and executed accurately according to a solid architectural plan. Because of its integrity, a building is able to stand strong through almost any kind of weather. God's integrity is the same way. He remains true to his plans and promises. God's goodness, mercy, and faithfulness are unshakable, no matter what the circumstance. The absolute integrity of God's character results in the righteousness of his actions toward you and others.

As you allow God to become more involved in your life, his righteousness begins to take hold in your own character. As your integrity grows in your relationship with God, it overflows into your relationships with others. The result is that even when relational storms begin to brew—when you face rejection, deceit, or betrayal—you

God's goodness, mercy, and faithfulness are unshakable, no matter what the circumstance.

have the strength and desire to stay true to God's plan. You can remain righteous in unrighteous surroundings. You can honor God with your life from the inside out.

Being righteous is fulfilling God's expectations for you. It is living up to who he created you to be. It's impossible to achieve this through self-effort; rather, you achieve this through God's Spirit and your will working together in harmony.

Jesus said, "The thing you should want most is God's kingdom and doing what God wants. Then all these other things you need will be given to you. So don't worry about tomorrow."

MATTHEW 6:33–34 NCV

First Things First

During the height of Jesus's popularity in Israel, crowds followed him everywhere, hungry for a word of insight or a touch of compassion. At that time, Jesus spoke at length (probably over several days) the words of what has come to be known as the Sermon on the Mount. Seated on a hill, Jesus shared practical lessons based on spiritual principles relating to everyday concerns. Jesus spoke about anger, revenge, and greed, the importance of building strong relationships, and God's provision for everyday needs, such as food and clothing.

Just like people today, the people of Jesus's time must have struggled to put all this into perspective. They must have longed to "get their priorities straight." Jesus's answer was simple: Put God first, and everything else will fall into place. This life principle is as powerful today as it was back then. Relationships,

> **Put God first, and everything else will fall into place. This life principle is as powerful today as it was back then.**

goals, responsibilities, and desires are constantly competing for your attention. Only by looking at them from God's perspective can you make wise decisions on how to use your time and energy in the way that makes the most positive and effective difference.

By continually choosing to live out your life in a way that reflects the priorities of God's kingdom in heaven, your concerns about things that are out of your control lose their grip on your heart. Your dependence on material provisions is transformed into a deep dependence on God. That's when you discover that whatever God provides is enough.

Throughout the Bible, dependence on God is always balanced by personal responsibility. As you do what God wants, he works through you to provide what you need.

Christ's anointing teaches you the truth on everything you need to know about yourself and him, uncontaminated by a single lie. Live deeply in what you were taught.

1 JOHN 2:27 MSG

Set Apart for a Purpose

In Old Testament times, pouring olive oil on something or someone was a sign that what was being anointed was being set apart for God's special use. High priests, rulers, and objects used in God's temple were all anointed and viewed as sacred. Jesus himself was often referred to as the "Anointed One," which is the meaning of *Messiah* in Hebrew and *Jesus* in Greek.

Through Jesus's sacrifice, you, too, have become an anointed one. Instead of being anointed with oil, you have

been anointed with God's own Spirit. You've been set apart for God's use in this world. In the Old Testament, God occasionally anointed people like David and Saul with the gift of his Spirit. But before Jesus

God's Spirit sets you apart and becomes your personal teacher and trainer.

came to earth, this kind of anointing wasn't permanent. God's Spirit could be taken away, as it was from the ruler Saul when Saul became lax in how he followed God.

Thanks to Jesus, the anointing of God's Spirit will never be taken away from you. God's Spirit sets you apart and becomes your personal teacher and trainer. He helps you understand Scripture, see things more clearly from God's perspective, and discern between God's truth and others' religious-sounding lies. However, you can experience only a part of God's Spirit while you're here on earth. That means your understanding of God, the Bible, and his ways is still imperfect. But God's Spirit will help lead you where you need to go in this life.

Although God's Spirit is your primary teacher, you can still learn a lot about God from other people, as long as they have his Spirit working in their lives so they can recognize truth.

Jesus said, "Be careful. Don't think these little children are worth nothing. I tell you that they have angels in heaven who are always with my Father in heaven."

Matthew 18:10–11 ncv

Lessons from a Child

As Jesus gained notoriety, so did his disciples. All the attention could have become a source of pride, which may be why the disciples asked Jesus who would be the greatest in his kingdom. Jesus's response was to call over a small child as an object lesson on humility. But Jesus didn't end this message with his admonition to become as open, unassuming, and teachable as a child. He also shared how important children were to God.

In the culture of the time, both women and children were viewed more as possessions than people. In contrast, Jesus treated every human being, regardless of sex, race, or age, as valuable. Though today children are generally treated with much higher regard than they were back then, they are still weak, helpless, and often unable to speak up for themselves. They depend on the adults around them for protection, provision, and love.

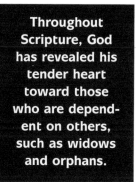

Throughout Scripture, God has revealed his tender heart toward those who are dependent on others, such as widows and orphans.

Throughout Scripture, God has revealed his tender heart toward those who are dependent on others, such as widows and orphans. Some believe that Jesus's lesson to his disciples means that every child has a guardian angel who watches out for his or her welfare. Whether that is true or not, one thing is certain. Children matter deeply to God. In turn, the way in which they are treated should matter deeply to you.

Whether you're a parent or not, daily life provides plenty of opportunities to share your love with a child. Being patient, approachable, and attentive when you're with kids is one way of sharing God's love.

Every good gift and every perfect gift is from above, and comes down from the Father of lights, with whom there is no variation or shadow of turning.

JAMES 1:17 NKJV

A Father's Favor

A gift is a tangible expression of love. That's why the best gifts you receive are usually given by those who know you well. These people know your likes and dislikes, your needs and your wants. They know your favorite color, perfect size, and what makes your heart sing. God is the ultimate giver of good gifts. His knowledge of who you really are is as limitless as his love for you.

The way God gives is as perfect as each gift he chooses to send your way. *Coming down* literally means "God's gifts keep on coming." There is no end to God's generosity to you.

In the same way that the sun keeps on shining even when the earth obstructs its light at night, God keeps on giving even when you don't notice what he's sending your way. And since God's character never wavers, you know his gift-giving habits will never change.

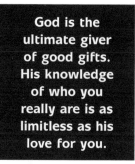

God is the ultimate giver of good gifts. His knowledge of who you really are is as limitless as his love for you.

You can trust he will continue to deliver wonderful surprises throughout eternity.

One of the devil's most effective lies is that God is not totally good, that he is holding out on you. It was this lie that Eve fell for in the Garden of Eden. Remembering the true nature of God and his gifts—that they are not only good, but perfect—will keep your heart filled with hope and gratitude, and your eyes open to blessings big and small that God chooses to send your way.

Not all of God's gifts seem perfect at first glance. Some are tough to accept wholeheartedly, like those that teach patience or humility. Trusting God's goodness will help you embrace every gift he sends.

Now that you are obedient children of God do not live as you did in the past. You did not understand, so you did the evil things you wanted. But be holy in all you do, just as God, the One who called you, is holy.

1 PETER 1:14–15 NCV

100 Percent Pure

The God of the Bible is unlike any false god people worshiped through the centuries. Early pagan gods were portrayed as bloodthirsty and sexually immoral. Roman gods were vengeful, adulterous, and deceitful. The God of Israel was, and is, absolutely holy. This means his character doesn't waver from a perfect moral standard. He's totally pure, true, and good.

The fact that God is holy is comforting, until you take a

look at your own moral standards in light of his. Even if in the world's eyes you live the life of a so-called saint, you still are not as perfectly holy as God. Yet the Bible seems to say that's exactly what God expects you to be.

To be holy is not a one-time transformation from depravity to perfection. It is more of a becoming. It is a lifetime of moment-by-moment decisions where you choose God's moral standards over what current culture says is acceptable. Only with the help of God's Spirit will you have the strength to consistently follow through and do the right thing. That doesn't mean you'll never make a mistake. Look at the life of the author of this letter, the apostle Peter. He tried to walk on water, but when he took his eyes off Jesus for just a moment, he instantly began to sink beneath the waves. The closer you grow to God, the easier it is to keep your eyes on him and the more your character will grow to resemble the holiness of his own.

> Only with the help of God's Spirit will you have the strength to consistently follow through and do the right thing.

Though you can make choices that honor God, you can't be truly holy without his help. Daily ask God to change your heart, as well as your actions, to be more pure.

Rejoice always, pray without ceasing, in everything give thanks; for this is the will of God in Christ Jesus for you.

1 THESSALONIANS 5:16–18 NKJV

The Circle of Joy

Anytime the Bible talks about God's will, what God wants for your life, it is time to pay close attention. There are three things God wants you to do all the time, in all circumstances—rejoice, pray, and say thank you. While each of these actions is important on its own, together they provide the secret to a joy-filled life.

In the original language, 1 Thessalonians 5:16 is the shortest verse in all Scripture. The charge to "rejoice always" seems to need no explanation, except that many life situations don't seem to be cause for rejoicing. However, while happiness ebbs and flows in relation to your situation, genuine joy remains constant regardless of what's going on around you. Your *feelings* of joy may rise and fall, but your reasons for joy remain steady and strong. That's because the joy the Bible speaks about is rooted in your relationship with God, not in your circumstance.

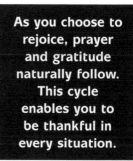

As you choose to rejoice, prayer and gratitude naturally follow. This cycle enables you to be thankful in every situation.

Rejoicing is putting that joy into action. You can express it through your attitude, actions, and communication with God and others. As you choose to rejoice, prayer and gratitude naturally follow. This cycle enables you to be thankful in every situation. That doesn't mean you're thankful *for* every situation. God doesn't ask you to thank him if you lose your job—or your child. Yet he provides reasons to be thankful even in the midst of tough times. Responding to those reasons deepens your joy, leading back to the never-ending circle of rejoicing, prayer, and thanks.

In Greek, "pray without ceasing" literally means "pray without intermission." That means there's never a major break in your communication with God. Expressing your joy in prayer helps keep your communication with God consistent.

Jesus said, "I pray for these followers, but I am also praying for all those who will believe in me because of their teaching. Father, I pray that they can be one. As you are in me and I am in you, I pray that they can also be one in us. Then the world will believe that you sent me."

JOHN 17:20–22 NCV

Learning to Live as One

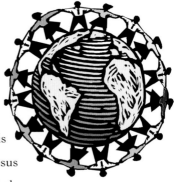

The night before Jesus died, you were on his mind. As Jesus's last supper with his disciples drew to a close, Jesus prayed aloud to his heavenly Father. He didn't pray about what lay ahead for him. Instead, he shared what his desires were for those he left behind.

Jesus's prayer for the unity of his disciples, both present and future, reveals some important truths about how God's church is supposed to function. Jesus's example of what the interaction between his followers should look like was the relationship between his Father and himself. The unique relationship of the Trinity, where the different attributes of the Father, Son, and Spirit all combine to make one God, is the perfect picture of unity. For humanity, this kind of supernatural bond isn't possible. The principle behind this example, however, is that people can work together as equals toward a common purpose while they retain their individuality.

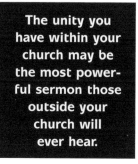

The unity you have within your church may be the most powerful sermon those outside your church will ever hear.

To work together, God's followers have to actually spend time together. As you choose to spend time with other people who believe in God, consider Jesus's prayer for you. Ask God for help in doing what you can to draw people together. Choose to build others up, instead of gossiping about their weaknesses. Search for common bonds, instead of arguing over petty differences. Strengthen your love by serving and readily forgiving. The unity you have within your church may be the most powerful sermon those outside your church will ever hear.

The book of Acts gives numerous examples of how Jesus's followers worked together after Jesus's resurrection, freely sharing their resources and their lives. Read Acts 2:26–47 for a glimpse of unity in action.

The LORD said to Joshua, "Always remember what is written in the Book of the Teachings. Study it day and night to be sure to obey everything that is written there. If you do this, you will be wise and successful in everything."

God's Secret to Success

Moses led the people of Israel out of slavery in Egypt, guided them safely through the parting of the Red Sea, brought them God's commandments from Mount Sinai, and led them through the desert to the boundaries of the land God had promised to give them. Then Moses died. Joshua was God's choice to lead the Israelites after Moses's death. Following in Moses's footsteps meant Joshua had big sandals to fill.

Before Joshua ventured into the Promised Land, God shared with him the secret to future success. God didn't offer tips on military strategy or promise Joshua he'd receive miraculous powers. God simply reminded Joshua to let Scripture influence his life. In the original Hebrew language, God encouraged Joshua to do more than just study his words. He told Joshua to *meditate* on them. This kind of meditation is different from what is practiced in Eastern religions. It means to allow God's words to deeply take root in your life by turning over God's truths in your mind and applying what you learn.

> The kind of success that results from allowing the Bible to come alive in your life differs from the world's definition of success. God isn't promising automatic health, wealth, and happiness as a reward for your obedience.

The kind of success that results from allowing the Bible to come alive in your life differs from the world's definition of success. God isn't promising automatic health, wealth, and happiness as a reward for your obedience. What he's saying is that by becoming better acquainted with Scripture, you'll succeed in filling the unique place he has set aside especially for you in this world.

⁓⁂◡

Take time to meditate on God's words to Joshua. Ask God to show you how he wants you to apply them to your own life situation.

One of the teachers of the law . . . asked
Jesus, "Which of the commands is most important?" Jesus answered, "The most important
command is this: 'Listen, people of Israel! The
Lord our God is the only Lord. Love the Lord
your God with all your heart, all your soul, all
your mind, and all your strength.' The second
command is this: 'Love your neighbor as you
love yourself.' There are no commands more
important than these."

MARK 12:28–31 NCV

Love Rules

Teachers
of the law, called scribes, were
Pharisees who spent much of
their time debating the meaning of
Scripture. One question they were frequently divided over was "Which of God's rules is most
important?" The scribes didn't debate just God's Ten
Commandments, they argued over 613 rules that they
derived from the first five books of the Bible, 248 "thou
shalts" and 365 "thou shalt nots." To settle this argument, or
perhaps to try to drag Jesus into the debate, one scribe

asked Jesus this popular loaded question.

Jesus began his answer by quoting the Shema: "Listen, people of Israel! The Lord our God is the only Lord." (The Shema is a traditional confession of faith that is still recited today every morning and evening by devout Jews.) After demonstrating his

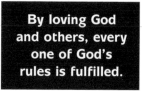

By loving God and others, every one of God's rules is fulfilled.

knowledge of tradition and Scripture, Jesus demonstrated his wisdom. He boiled down the Ten Commandments, and even the 613 precepts, to one life-changing principle: love.

Instead of focusing on rules, Jesus told the scribe to focus on relationship. By loving God and others, every one of God's rules is fulfilled. Loving God with everything you are—with all your emotions, intellect, and energy—is what gives you the desire and the wisdom you need to love others well. Anytime you're in doubt as to what God wants you to do in a given situation, ask yourself, "Right now, how can I love God and others best?"

The word *neighbor* literally means "the one near you." As you go through your day, consider how many neighbors you encounter, both physically and emotionally, and what you can do to love them well.

Jesus said to her, "I am the resurrection and the life. He who believes in Me, though he may die, he shall live. And whoever lives and believes in Me shall never die."

JOHN 11:25–26 NKJV

Life-and-Death Issues

Martha had a firm grasp of reality. She knew her brother, Lazarus, was dead and buried. She also knew that for some reason Jesus didn't come as soon as she and her sister, Mary, had called to ask for his help. Martha believed in a heavenly resurrection, but Martha's faith in Jesus's power and love was so strong she believed there was still hope for her brother.

That's when Jesus made a bold statement. As he'd done previously, Jesus referred to himself with the words "I am," a name reserved by the Jews for God alone. When

Jesus spoke about how someone may die, then live, yet whoever lives will never die, Jesus wasn't playing semantic word

games. He was talking about two different kinds of death—physical and
spiritual. Though everyone faces
physical death, not everyone needs to
face spiritual death. Faith in Jesus and
his resurrection raises a person's spiritual life up from the grave, instantly
and permanently.

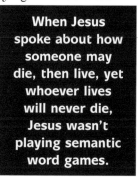

When Jesus spoke about how someone may die, then live, yet whoever lives will never die, Jesus wasn't playing semantic word games.

By being both the resurrection and the life, Jesus could
do more than simply restore life. He had the power to maintain it, to return it to what God originally designed it to be.
Jesus demonstrated this power in a visible way by bringing
Lazarus back to life. Although some day Lazarus would die
again physically, thanks to his belief in Jesus Lazarus never
had to face death spiritually. He would be with God throughout his life on earth and beyond.

⌐∭◦

You cannot determine the day of your death, but you can
determine the day you truly come to life by believing
in Jesus. Consider what resurrection means to you in a spiritual sense.

If you need wisdom—if you want to know what God wants you to do—ask him, and he will gladly tell you.

JAMES 1:5 NLT

Just Ask

Doing what God wants you to do is a wonderful thing. It honors God, adds joy to your life, and can make a positive difference in the world. However, knowing what God wants you to do in any given situation isn't always clear. Reading the Bible can give you some general guidelines, but knowing how to apply what you learn takes more than just diligence and good intentions. It takes discernment.

Discernment is the ability to make wise decisions when you're facing difficult circumstances. God holds an endless supply of the wisdom you need to be discerning. In the original language, the author James used words that identify God with a banker. James explained that when your own account of wisdom falls short, God will loan you some from his abundant supply. Unlike stingy moneylenders who would belittle those who needed to rely on their services, James said

> **Reading the Bible can give you some general guidelines, but knowing how to apply what you learn takes more than just diligence and good intentions. It takes discernment.**

that God is more than happy to share all of what he has with you—at no interest.

This isn't a promise that God will give you a windfall of wisdom the first time you ask for it. The word *ask* actually means "to keep on asking." By continually turning to God for wisdom every time you need help, you will learn to discern the right thing to do when the pressure is on.

—⟩⟩⟩

Instead of God giving you an exact blueprint of what he wants for your life, he draws you closer to him by supplying what you need when you need it—as you rely on him.

He used his servant body to carry our sins to the Cross so we could be rid of sin, free to live the right way. His wounds became your healing.

1 PETER 2:24 MSG

The Ultimate Cure

People go to extremes to find healing in this life. They will travel across the country, and even across the world, searching for a cure for what they have been told is incurable. They will try radical treatments and undergo outlandish procedures, hoping for a miracle. When word of Jesus's miraculous power started circulating throughout Palestine, people flocked to him, pleading for physical healing. Over and over again he responded to their cries. He healed blindness, leprosy, mental illness, paralysis—and even death. However, that healing wasn't permanent.

Eventually each one of those people would die.

The apostle Peter had repeatedly witnessed Jesus curing the incurable. But he understood that Jesus came to offer more than temporary physical or emotional healing. Jesus came to offer an eternal cure for physical and spiritual death. When Peter talked about Jesus's *wounds*, the original Greek word is singular. There was one specific wound that offered heal-

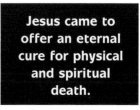

Jesus came to offer an eternal cure for physical and spiritual death.

ing. That was Jesus's death on the cross. That wound didn't begin the healing process. It finished it.

There are times when miraculous healing still occurs in this life, when tumors disappear and cancer suddenly goes into remission. However, through what happened on a wooden cross two thousand years ago, you have received permanent healing for something more important than your physical health. You have been given a new life, one that has been cured of the finality of death.

The book of 1 Peter was written to slaves who knew what it was like to receive beatings and wounds they didn't deserve. Take some time today to thank Jesus for what he suffered for you.

All the angels are spirits who serve God and are sent to help those who will receive salvation.

HEBREWS 1:14 NCV

Invisible Servants

Angels are "in" today. There are books about encounters with angels, jewelry designs that symbolize angelic protection, and popular catchphrases claiming that "friends are angels without wings." Back in Jesus's day, people were as intrigued by the mystery of angelic beings as they are today. After Jesus's death, there was even some speculation that Jesus wasn't really God, but instead a powerful angel sent from heaven.

The unknown author of Hebrews wanted to set the record straight by putting angels, and Jesus, in their proper place. He began by tying together Old Testament verses that talk about Jesus, Scripture where God declared his Son equal to him in position as King and Lord. Then the author explained the purpose of angels in God's plan of creation, as servants of both God and the people who believe in him.

Throughout Scripture, angels have served as messengers, guardians, and comforters. Although the Bible mentions them frequently enough to ensure that God wants people to know of their existence, God remains silent on the details of what they are truly like.

> **Angels are real, and at God's command they are helping you in ways you may not be aware of.**

What can be gleaned from a few brief descriptions in the Old Testament is that angels are much more like fearsome warriors than ephemeral creatures in gossamer gowns with white wings and golden harps. Angels are real, and at God's command they are helping you in ways you may not be aware of.

One way angels serve God is by serving those he loves, which includes you. Although angels are powerful, they are not meant to be worshiped. Only God is worthy of that honor.

If you confess with your mouth that Jesus is Lord and believe in your heart that God raised him from the dead, you will be saved. For it is by believing in your heart that you are made right with God, and it is by confessing with your mouth that you are saved.

ROMANS 10:9–10 NLT

Totally in Agreement with God

In the Bible, the word *confession* is rich with meaning. In the Hebrew language of the Old Testament, *confession* meant at the same time "to praise God" and "to admit your sins." One could not be separated from the other. Personal confession was often done in public through song or prayer. Personal confession was a time of repentance and rejoicing intertwined.

In the Greek language of the New Testament, *confess* meant "to say the same thing." To confess that Jesus is Lord meant that you were saying the same thing about Jesus that God did, agreeing with everything Scripture had to say about who he was and what he did for you. Whether you were confessing

Personal confession was often done in public through song or prayer.

your sins or confessing that Jesus is God, in essence you were saying, "I agree with what God says is true."

In the early church, no Jew or Gentile would publicly say that Jesus was God unless he or she truly believed it. Because of the threat of persecution, people were probably much less likely to base their faith on their feelings than on a carefully considered intellectual conclusion. Once you come to the same life-changing conclusion as the people in the early church, talking about what you believe is a natural reaction to understanding what God has done for you.

The author's words in the original language speak about confession and belief as ongoing activities. Confessing and believing should play an active part in the everyday experience of those who choose to trust God.

Regard prisoners as if you were in prison with them. Look on victims of abuse as if what happened to them had happened to you.

Hebrews 13:3 msg

Empathy in Action

In the early church, it was commonplace for people who chose to follow Jesus to suffer relationally, financially, and physically for what they believed. They often lost their property, their position, and sometimes even their lives. Although no one knows for sure who the author of the book of Hebrews was, one thing is certain—he was aware of the persecution that was going on all around him.

While Jesus was here on earth, he warned those who followed him that people would persecute them, just as they had him. After Jesus's death, that persecution intensified. It

may seem today that people are more accepting and that persecution is a thing of the past. However, that's not true for much of the world.

There are still people who suffer for their beliefs the same way the early Christians did. The words to the Hebrews are a wake-up call for every generation. If you truly want to empathize and identify with those who are facing persecution (which is who the author of Hebrews

> **God may choose to use you to help answer the prayer of someone around the world.**

was specifically talking about), you will do more than just feel sorry for them. You will put your empathy into action. A good place to begin is with prayer. Ask God to protect people who are persecuted, to provide them with the strength and courage they need to face their struggles. As you pray, God may lead you to take social action. God may choose to use you to help answer the prayer of someone around the world.

—

Become more aware of the persecution going on in the world by logging on to persecution.com. The nonprofit, interdenominational organization The Voice of the Martyrs provides ways for you to put Hebrews 13:3 into action.

Jesus said, "Those who are well have no need of a physician, but those who are sick. I have not come to call the righteous, but sinners, to repentance."

LUKE 5:31–32 NKJV

Jesus Makes House Calls

Jesus had asked several fishermen to follow him and become disciples. However, Jesus's most recent choice for a disciple was raising more than a few eyebrows among Jewish religious leaders. Matthew was a tax collector, and tax collectors were despised by Jews and Gentiles alike. The rate of taxes people had to pay was vague, so it was easy for tax collectors to charge people more than they should. Then the tax collectors would use the excess they received to live extravagant lifestyles. For the Jews, the fact that a Jewish tax collector would even associate with Gentiles was itself a problem. Even if Matthew was an honest, God-fearing Jew, he was viewed by his peers as a disreputable sinner.

The Pharisee challenged Jesus's association with Matthew—and Jesus's attending a party at Matthew's house with other sinners just like him. Jesus's response was a bit tongue-in-cheek. He spoke to the Pharisees' view of themselves, that they were righteous and spiritually healthy, which they were not. By doing so, he emphasized how his time should be spent with those who needed his help most, instead of with those who didn't recognize their need.

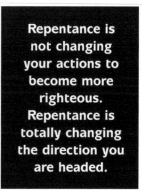

Repentance is not changing your actions to become more righteous. Repentance is totally changing the direction you are headed.

Jesus called people not just to follow him, but to repent. Repentance is totally changing the direction you are headed. It is allowing God to change your mind and heart to be more in line with his own. Once you do that, a change in your actions, plans, and attitudes will naturally follow.

Matthew's change of direction was so radical that he wound up writing part of the Bible, the Gospel of Matthew. Through God, your life change can be just as dramatic and significant.

In Christ, there is no difference between Jew and Greek, slave and free person, male and female. You are all the same in Christ Jesus.

GALATIANS 3:28 NCV

Uniquely Equal

During Jesus's time, the culture was filled with social division. Jews kept their distance from Gentiles. Slaves were treated like property instead of people. A woman's worth was often determined by her ability to bear children. She wasn't allowed to study the Scriptures or own property. Men and women who weren't acquainted wouldn't dare speak in public, and even those who knew one another well would never have any kind of physical contact outside their own home.

Jesus changed all that. He spoke with women, taught them, and encouraged them to teach others. He took those who were ill by the hand, regardless of their gender. Jesus conversed with Jews and Gentiles, servants and leaders, tax collectors and prostitutes. He even dared to touch lepers, who were considered the lowest of all outcasts by the rest of society. Jesus treated every person

Jesus conversed with Jews and Gentiles, servants and leaders, tax collectors and prostitutes.

with dignity and compassion. That's because he knew who each individual really was—a person created in the image of God.

The ways people look, act, and live are incredibly diverse, but each one has the same value in God's eyes. If racial, social, and gender distinctions don't hinder God's love for individuals, they shouldn't hinder yours. Ask God to help you see people as he does, worthy of your love, your time, and your wholehearted acceptance.

You can disagree with people's opinions, beliefs, or lifestyles and still love and accept them as individuals. Read through the book of John, taking special note of how Jesus does exactly that.

J esus said, "These things I have spoken to you, that in Me you may have peace. In the world you will have tribulation; but be of good cheer, I have overcome the world."

JOHN 16:33 NKJV

The Straight Scoop

When you want to calm people's anxiety, elaborating on their current problems and then reminding them that more trouble is headed their way is usually not the recommended modus operandi. But that's exactly the approach Jesus took with his disciples at the Last Supper. He explained that he would be leaving them, that there was a betrayer in their midst, and that all of them would abandon him in his time of need. Jesus told the disciples they'd be hated and persecuted and would even face death because of their faith in him.

Jesus's telling his disciples to "be of good cheer" after all of this sounds like a coach's telling his losing team to "look on the bright side." However, in ancient Greek, telling someone to "cheer up" was not a verbal pat on the back. It meant to take courage in the face of danger. Jesus didn't offer his closest friends

> **Jesus didn't offer his closest friends pessimistic predictions or optimistic platitudes. He simply told them the truth.**

pessimistic predictions or optimistic platitudes. He simply told them the truth.

Part of this truth was that both peace and victory could be theirs even when the world seemed to be falling apart all around them. Jesus challenged his disciples to be overcomers rather than to be overcome by their problems. Just like the disciples, you will have trouble in this life. Jesus guaranteed it. However, by focusing on God's power, promises, and presence in your life, you, too, can find the courage and comfort you need to face any trouble that comes your way.

The Bible never sugarcoats the fact that life isn't easy. Its overall message, however, is one of hope and healing. You can always trust God to be honest about the good and the bad.

W hen we were baptized, we were buried with Christ and shared his death. So, just as Christ was raised from the dead by the wonderful power of the Father, we also can live a new life.

ROMANS 6:4 NCV

Tempered for Transformation

In ancient Greece, a metalsmith "baptized" hot iron by dipping it into water. This act tempered the metal, strengthening it and helping set the specific shape the smith had chosen for the iron to take. In some respects, that's what baptism does for those who believe in God. It tempers them. It helps strengthen how closely they identify with God and their new form of life in a public yet personal way.

The New Testament records many instances of baptism, including Jesus's own baptism in the Jordan River. The Greek word for *baptize* means "to immerse." That's what early Christians did. Early Christians were immersed in water as an outward sign of the inward change God had brought into their lives. Time and again in Scripture, one of the first things people did after choosing to believe in God was to ask to be baptized. They wanted to demonstrate to God and to those around them that they were serious about their newfound faith.

Baptism is a symbolic illustration of what Jesus went through to bring about your new spiritual life. Being lowered into the water symbolizes Jesus's death and burial in a tomb.

> **Christians were immersed in water as an outward sign of the inward change God had brought into their lives.**

Being raised from the water is a picture of Jesus's rising from the dead and beginning a new kind of life, one that doesn't end in death. According to the Bible, baptism doesn't wash away your sins or gain you entrance into heaven. What it does is demonstrate your desire to fully live the life God created you to live.

⟨⟩

Different churches have different traditions about how and when people are baptized. Why you want to be baptized, and not the method in which your baptism takes place, is what matters to God.

In all these things we are more than conquerors through Him who loved us. For I am persuaded that neither death nor life, nor angels nor principalities nor powers, nor things present nor things to come, nor height nor depth, nor any other created thing, shall be able to separate us from the love of God which is in Christ Jesus our Lord.

ROMANS 8:37–39 NKJV

Conquerors *Extraordinaire*

Consider what people dread most in life. The list could include things like war, betrayal, famine, abandonment, poverty, pain, and death. In his letter to the Romans, the apostle Paul presented a similar list. However, what Paul addressed as the most serious of all concerns was that facing tumultuous times could build a wall between God and those who believed in him, that turmoil could cut people off from God's love.

Jesus's followers in Rome were facing difficult times firsthand. Paul offered them comfort, encouragement, and hope by following his list of worst-case scenarios with the best news he could deliver. No hardship in life could prevent God's love from reaching them and leading them to victory. When Paul wrote "I am persuaded," he meant "I'm absolutely convinced. You can stake your faith and your life on this fact."

The assurance of victory God promises through the words of Paul doesn't mean you'll get every job you apply for, always end your financial year in the black, or never contract a fatal disease. God's promise of victory is specific to the

> **God's promise of victory is specific to the role he's given you to fill in this life.**

role he's given you to fill in this life. When you're faced with hard times, it won't be your intelligence, your talents, or your perseverance that will eventually ensure your victory. It will be God's love, working through you to keep you close to God's side and to help you rise above whatever has you down.

Facing hard times can lead you to become more than victorious because hard times make you depend more on God and on his strength than on your own.

It's in Christ that we find out who we are and what we are living for. Long before we first heard of Christ and got our hopes up, he had his eye on us, had designs on us for glorious living, part of the overall purpose he is working out in everything and everyone.

EPHESIANS 1:11–12 MSG

This Is Your Life

Why are you here? Is there life after death? What is truth? Is there really a universal code for right and wrong? Does your life make a difference in the big picture of history? People have debated questions like these for thousands of years. The answers to them all lie in understanding who Jesus really is. The better you know Jesus, the better you'll know yourself and understand your place and purpose in the world.

In the original language, Jesus's "overall purpose" speaks to God's ultimate plan for the world. It's his big picture, in which you play one important, unique part. Jesus's design for you relates to his desire for your individual life. This is what Jesus wants to see happen. How you respond to Jesus makes a difference in how well Jesus's desire for you is fulfilled.

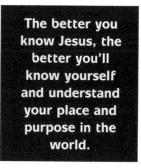

The better you know Jesus, the better you'll know yourself and understand your place and purpose in the world.

According to science, one way of determining life is by observing movement and growth. The same is true spiritually. As you act on what you understand about Jesus, you'll mature more fully into who you were created to be. By reading the Bible, spending time with God in prayer, and doing what you feel God wants you to do, you will come alive in the deepest, most authentic sense of the word. The true meaning of life will become evident in you.

Consider the ways in which knowing God helps you know more about yourself. Spend some time today just talking to God about your unique place in this world.

Your word is a lamp to
my feet and a light to
my path.

PSALM 119:105 NKJV

Jesus said to those Jews who believed Him, "If you abide in My word, you are My disciples indeed. And you shall know the truth, and the truth shall make you free."

JOHN 8:31–32 NKJV